Western Philosophy Made Easy

A Personal Search for Meaning

D1188648

Western Philosophy Made Easy

A Personal Search for Meaning

Dennis Waite

BOOKS

Winchester, UK
Washington, USA

First published by iff Books, 2018
iff Books is an imprint of John Hunt Publishing Ltd., No. 3 East Street, Alresford,
Hampshire SO24 9EE, UK
office1@jhpbooks.net
www.johnhuntpublishing.com
www.iff-books.com

For distributor details and how to order please visit the 'Ordering' section on our website.

ISBN: 978 1 78535 778 7
978 1 78535 779 4 (ebook)
Library of Congress Control Number: 2017946770

A CIP catalogue record for this book is available from the British Library.

Design: Stuart Davies

Printed and bound by CPI Group (UK) Ltd, Croydon, CR0 4YY, UK

We operate a distinctive and ethical publishing philosophy in
all areas of our business, from our global network of authors to
production and worldwide distribution.

Contents

Background

The principal reason why people begin to read books on Philosophy is that they are deeply dissatisfied with their lives. They have discovered that worldly pleasures do not bring happiness and they start to think about meaning and purpose. They may consider looking for answers in either religion or philosophy. Which they choose depends upon their upbringing and education. If parents have told them that there is a god (or gods), who 'watches over' the world and our own lives (whether or not there is any 'interference' in these), then he or she may well turn to their faith for some explanation and guidance. If not (or if any such ideas have been overturned by independent consideration) then they must have recourse to their own thought and intellect, guided by those who have gone through this process before and recorded their conclusions in books.

I had a very intensive education. For seven years, I attended a school that was a significant distance from home, so that, each day, I had a three-hour return journey, plus a couple of hours of homework, in addition to the school day itself. I did not have time (or opportunity) for any 'worldly pleasures.' University provided plenty of opportunities, of course, but I had never acquired the social skills to take advantage of them. By the time I began work, I was pretty dissatisfied with life and ripe for beginning my own 'search for meaning.'

This began in earnest when I began attending the School of Economic Science (SES) in London, in response to the 'Course of Philosophy' lectures that they advertised on the Underground. I stayed there for a couple of years until they wanted me to part with a week's salary to be initiated into Transcendental Meditation. But at that time, they were still mainly influenced by the Eastern mystic Ouspensky, and their teaching was a bit weird to say the least, scarcely representative of Western philosophy.

After a break to get married, have a child, get divorced and remarry, I returned to SES in the mid-1980s, since this was still the only source I had found which gave some slight promise of providing answers to my 'angst.' I stayed until around 1998, by which time I had been a tutor with the school for a number of years.

After rejoining SES, I made a number of attempts to discover the source of their teaching. I looked in bookstores and libraries and searched philosophy books. It was this process that provided the background knowledge presented in this book. But, despite my energetic searching, it was quite a few years before I actually discovered the main influence for the school's teaching. It was the non-dual, Hindu philosophy of Advaita Vedanta. But I am getting ahead of myself. First – the subject of this book – I want to look at the extent to which Western philosophers of the past two thousand plus years have provided guidance as to how to live, together with justification for such guidance (in the form of meaning and purpose) and some reasoned presentation of the nature of reality.

What Western Philosophers Have Said

Philosophers used not to limit their investigation to those areas that we now think of as philosophy. Aristotle for example wrote books on physics, biology, mathematics, psychology, politics and meteorology, to mention just a few. Their interests ranged across the entire spectrum of human endeavor. It should not be too surprising, then, to find that many philosophers do not seem specifically to have addressed the questions that concern those individuals trying to make sense of their lives – there were simply too many other diverting subjects to investigate. Nevertheless, since the question of what we ought to do in order to achieve fulfillment and happiness is rather more important than most, it is perhaps surprising that it seems so difficult to discover clear guidance from this intellectual elite.

What follows is a very brief overview of the subject from the early Greeks up to the modern day, in a strictly nonacademic presentation (with many of the usual anecdotal comments!). I have tried to pick out any ideas that relate in some degree to our search for meaning. Many philosophers are much better known for their work in other areas and I have said little or nothing about them. I am not philosophically educated and my knowledge of history is atrocious. If you want to learn about the history of Western philosophy, there are many, excellent, readable books available (even if few people actually read them!). The questions that interest me are those that must have existed ever since man first looked further than where his next meal was coming from. I will be concluding that the answers provided by a particular Eastern philosophy are far more pertinent and helpful but it would be presumptuous, to say the least, to suggest that the answers given by that philosophy are in some way more complete, accurate or 'true' than those provided by Western philosophers without at least being aware of the nature of what these philosophers have said.

Philosophical Counseling

Philosophical Counseling is a relatively new discipline that has sprung up to serve those who are suffering from problems that are believed to have been caused by lack of knowledge or understanding rather than because they are mentally disturbed. They need informed advice rather than medical treatment. Once, such people might have visited their priest, local vicar or village elder. Until the advent of philosophical counselors, there were few options. In the latter part of the twentieth century, it became fashionable to visit a psychotherapist, if one could afford it. At the cheaper end of the market, there were always 'agony aunts' and fortune-tellers. The most likely option, however, was simply to talk things over with one's parents or with friends down at the pub. It seems that, in the past, all of those who might have provided this sort of counseling service would have been likely to be biased in some way. Perhaps they were attached to a specific religion or to some other system of belief or simply to their own habits of thought, acquired through their particular upbringing and experience.

There are usually experts available for consultation on the more mundane aspects of life, such as how to cope with financial problems, sue or divorce someone and so on. And there are those who can help with serious illness or bereavement. But when it comes to questions about who we really are and what we ought to do with our lives, it seems we just have to sort them out for ourselves. Philosophical Counseling aims to change that by providing independent advice founded upon knowledge accumulated by the best thinkers of the past few thousand years.

One of the principal aims of Philosophy, after all, must be to discover how to live one's life optimally, whether or not it actually claims that there is a purpose as such. Trained in logic and the application of reason to problems, philosophers are ideally placed to be able to resolve personal conflicts, clarify contradicting values and generally enable one to put things into perspective and establish a course of action. In a sense, the problem could be described as a disease of the intellect, with the philosopher, skilled in this domain, able to establish the symptoms through discussion, diagnose the underlying problem of misunderstanding and provide a remedy by restating the difficulty, clarifying terms and indicating how the situation might be resolved – what the twentieth century philosopher Wittgenstein called "untying the knots in our thinking."

Everyone knows that talking over their problems with an uninvolved friend can help shed light on the issues and show possible ways forward to resolution. Friends are not usually trained in disciplines such as logic and ethics, however, so such help is somewhat haphazard. If help is not available in the early stages, worry may lead to stress or breakdown and then the only recourse is to psychiatric help. Philosophical counseling aims to provide help in the early stages, while one's mind is still actively seeking solutions rather than resorting to despair and resignation. And, if your problems relate to discovering a meaning in life, differentiating between 'pleasant' and 'good' or deciding whether your ambitions are the 'right' ones, then you definitely need a philosopher. In this sense, then, this book could be regarded as a preliminary, overview 'counseling' session.

Branches of Philosophy

There are many branches of philosophy. Epistemology is all about knowledge – types of knowledge, objects and sources of knowledge, knowledge and certainty, belief, doubt, causation and so on – a huge subject in its own right. Some philosophers restrict their studies to aspects of this, such as the Empiricists, who believe that our knowledge is derived from the senses, or the Rationalists who argue that we can reason our way to new knowledge that was not previously directly accessible. Logic is a realm in its own right, as is the philosophy of language or political philosophy. The Philosophy of mind is another area to which people devote their lives and one which has much popular appeal today.

Ethics and moral philosophy is yet another very large branch and the one that looks as though it ought to be the most relevant to our lives. A teacher will tell you that it is important for you to listen to all that she says, to read and study in order, ultimately, to pass your exams. But then this is her job and both of you are functioning within the context of a society that automatically values these things. But is education good in itself? Why should learning about a particular subject (that in all probability will be of no use to you for the rest of your life) be something on which you should expend effort? The teacher presupposes that education is a good thing; ethics allows you to question this.

Not all philosophers who have written on the subject of ethics have specifically asked the question of what we ought to do with our lives. Concentrating more on the purpose of morality itself, they have ended up considering questions such as the ideal society, how people can live together optimally and so on, leaving our personal motivations and objectives to our own individual conscience. And this is understandable to some extent. After all, why should I listen to someone *else* telling me how I ought to act in order to make *my* life feel fulfilled? The answer is that it is likely that someone who has deeply investigated such questions may just have thought of aspects that you haven't considered and may have reached conclusions that you will find helpful. If the serious consideration of such questions requires that we also look into all of these subjects, then perhaps we are perfectly justified in seeking the guidance of experts.

So, even within the limited realm of what we now call philosophy, it is clear that it would not be possible for anyone to address all of these subjects in other than a cursory manner and it is inevitable that interests will tend in a specific direction. Here, then, is a further reason why many of the major philosophers do not seem to have anything particularly helpful to say to someone looking for personal advice. (A proviso needs to be given at this point that it is quite possible that relevant things *were* said by them but outside of my hearing!)

Conversely just because a topic does not seem directly relevant, it should not be assumed that we can ignore it. It would not be reasonable to suppose that something so fundamental as the purpose of our life could be studied in isolation. Take the question 'What should I do?', for example. We need to investigate what we mean by 'I' – who am I exactly? Until we feel that we know the answer to this, the original question is not meaningful. We need to ask about the nature of the world in which we are proposing to act. We need to be sure that we are able to choose our course of action, otherwise the original question is somewhat irrelevant, and we need to know something about what it means to act. These are all questions of Metaphysics (meaning those things that come after physics). And we do need to know a little about what it means to 'know' anything and the means by which we find things out. All of these seem to be required before we can begin to ask about subjects such as 'good' (and 'God') and about the reasons for acting in one way rather than another. So it does look as if a question about one major aspect of our life will soon draw in many of the other questions of philosophy, like it or not.

Metaphysics, as the study of the questions of 'life, the universe and everything' is known, fell out of vogue in the twentieth century, when the attitude arose that most of what had previously been thought to be intransigent problems were not really problems at all but arose through our inability to formulate the problem correctly. Once we used language properly, it was argued, the difficulties would disappear. Many recent philosophers have not even addressed the sort of fundamental questions that arise for the 'seeker of truth.' In this respect there is a similarity with science. There was a time when an enquiring mind could range over the entire domain of what is now thought of as 'science', becoming expert in many areas and making new discoveries. The amount of material that was written down and accepted as proven was minimal. Over the past few centuries, the rate of investigation and discovery has accelerated and it is now possible to conduct novel research in only a tiny area of specialization. In the 3rd century BC, Aristotle's multi-disciplined enquiries have already been noted. By the 20th century, most of the philosophy in England was devoted to analyzing the meanings of sentences!

Many philosophical ideas seem abstruse and intellectual and it is not surprising that a metaphysician has been described as "a man who goes into a dark cellar at midnight, without a light, looking for a black cat that is not there." But clearly, if you become aware of some of these ideas and believe them, then it does become necessary to modify your life accordingly, if you are not to feel that you are missing the point completely. More importantly, how can you become aware of them if you do not make the effort to find out? You owe it to yourself to make some effort to establish what has been discovered or conjectured by those who have devoted their lives to such investigations. If you fail to do this now, then how may you feel in later life when 'the end' is getting nearer and you no longer have the time to make the enquiry?

The name given to the branch of Philosophy that deals with judgments about the (nonmoral) 'values' of things is called 'Axiology.' It is usually regarded as a branch of Ethics, which itself is more generally concerned with what we *ought* to do or not do. Once you ask what *you* ought to do, you need to consider how this might affect others, whether it is moral or just, if it is actually possible to answer the question and how we could know that it was the *right* answer in any objective sense. Clearly, acting in such a way as to help others is not necessarily going to make our own lives easier or more pleasurable. Presuming that the main reason for acting at all is the pursuance of happiness, we are obliged to ask what that word actually means. We would tend to claim that it was not possible to be truly happy in conditions of poverty or oppression so that politics have to be taken into consideration. If we think that there might be some purpose to our existence or even an afterlife and/or a God overlooking our activities, then we will have to take into account metaphysical considerations. It all becomes very complicated!

Key Philosophers

Pre-Socratic Philosophers

There are a number of these whose names you will still encounter, some of whose ideas are able to influence philosophers two millennia later. Understandably, not much remains of their writings from five or six centuries BC. Most were interested in the more metaphysical aspects, though since this differentiation had not yet been made, they probably considered that their subject was rather 'natural science.' "What is the nature of the universe?" they asked. The answer was that they were mostly materialists – they believed that it was made of matter rather than mind or spirit. But they all believed that the most important thing that we could do with our lives was to study philosophy... but then they would, wouldn't they?

Heraclitus is one of the better known, famous for his observation that the river that we step into for a second time is effectively not the same as the one into which we stepped the first time. The world has always and will always exist but *"was ever, is now, and ever shall be, an ever-living Fire,"* constantly changing. And things that appear to be opposites are really just extremes of a single thing, like the north and south poles of a magnet. Our phenomenal world is in a constant state of flux and the key to understanding it is introspection, looking inwards to 'find' ourselves where there is stability and changelessness. *"All things come out of one,"* he said, *"and the one out of all things; but the many have less reality than the one, which is God."* He was what we would now probably call a 'mystic' and the few fragments of his writing that remain are obscure, to say the least! But these cryptic comments influenced later philosophers such as Hegel and Nietzsche, as well as others such as TS Eliot, for example, whose wonderful poem "The Four Quartets" quotes him directly in several places.

A disciple of Heraclitus, called Cratylus, took the idea of

continual change to its limits. He said that it was not even possible to hold a discussion since, by the time one came to answer a question, the person asking the question, the one answering and even the words and meanings would all have changed. So all he could do when asked something was wiggle a finger to indicate that he had heard, though whom he thought he was responding to is unclear!

Parmenides was also influential, especially with respect to logic. He believed that our senses deceive us as regards the nature of objects. There are not *many* things but only 'the One', which is infinite and indivisible, present everywhere (and spherical!). He disagreed totally with Heraclitus, saying that there is never any change. There must *be* things, since we think of them and name them and, since we can do this at any moment, they must always exist. Conversely, it is simply not possible to think or speak of things that do not exist. The real always exists and is unchanging. That which changes must not exist and cannot be part of the real. The arguments and conclusions are not very clear and no one is being asked to accept the statements as made above! They are noted to give the flavor of thought relating to what would become known as the metaphysical. But it should be noted that Parmenides is still influential, and his philosophy does contain elements of the Hindu philosophy of Advaita, which I mentioned earlier and will be promoting later. In particular Raphael, who has written commentaries on a number of texts attributed to Shankara (the 8th century philosopher who was most influential in systematizing Advaita), was much influenced by him. Also, there is an organization called the Parmenides Traditional Philosophy Foundation in New York.

Socrates

The early Greek philosophers had been concerned with such things as discovering the primary constituent of matter and the governing principles of the universe. The Sophists were more interested in practical aspects of man's behavior but concentrated on such things as oratory and argument. It was not until Socrates that ethical questions were asked – What ought we to do? What is the meaning of justice and truth? What is the 'good'? He devoted his life to exposing ignorance and endeavoring to lead people towards knowledge of their real nature. He claimed that it was necessary to define exactly what we meant by concepts such as 'justice' in order that we could know how to live. He did not write anything himself but Plato, who made Socrates the hero of his own books, recorded much of Socrates' thinking in the form of dialogues with his fellow Athenians.

Plato believed that there was a right way to behave – the 'good' – and that if a person knew what this was he would automatically act in this way. He thought that it was possible to find out this 'good' in the same way that one might discover a mathematical truth. He further believed that there was only *one* 'good'; it was not dependent upon personal desires or opinions. It might require a trained philosopher to find out the relevant truths but, once we have understood them, we will automatically behave in the right way and be optimally happy, even when confronted by people who, not having the benefit of this knowledge, act otherwise. It is hardly surprising that subsequent development of his philosophy, in what is called 'Neo-Platonism', was very influential upon Christianity.

Our fundamental beliefs regarding our nature are bound to influence our thoughts and behavior. If we firmly believe, like Plato, that this world and its pleasures are transient and that we have eternal souls that belong to another, perfect world then we cannot accord the same significance to what happens here and now as would the atheist, who believes that this body and its experiences in this lifetime are all that there is. Instead we are obliged to try to find out more about the 'good' so that we maximize the benefits to ourselves and others in this life and prepare our souls for the eternity after bodily death. Inevitably, we would find little to satisfy us in the temporary pleasures of this ultimately unreal world. So, at least, the theory goes. You may think that the hedonistic lifestyle of the intellectual elite in the time of the classical Greeks, and their tendency to fixate on beautiful male youths, suggests that not many actually adhered to these principles.

Plato

Socrates is famous for claiming that "the unexamined life is not worth living." If we simply go through our lives seeking pleasures for their own sake without ever looking for some sense of purpose and meaning, then we might as well not have existed. The hedonist's retort to this is that, if we spend all of our lives searching for significance and fail to find any (whether or not there actually *is* some), then we have wasted our opportunity to enjoy it while we are able. The fact that many claim that there is a purpose, and that they themselves have realized this, is not really any help. Most of such people will be held by us to be deluded religious fanatics and their opinions will carry little weight. If there is meaning then it does seem that we must discover it for ourselves, perhaps by systematically examining all of the claims and deciding whether they are in any way justified.

Plato also had much to say on morality. What *ought* we to do? Are some actions good and others bad? Should we act solely to benefit ourselves or (try to) take into account the feelings of others? Our natural inclinations must be to further our own interests. As Darwin pointed out much later, we are biologically driven to survive and prosper, passing on the genes that have helped us to do so to the next generation. Those members of the species that are genetically ill-suited to doing this simply die out. But Plato said that we also have a need to form societies. Each of us does not have all of the skills needed to provide an optimum environment. If someone is especially good at building, for example, it makes sense for others to utilize his skills and to provide something of their own in exchange, perhaps hunting, cooking or protection. Once groups begin to form in this way, it becomes necessary to agree on codes of behavior for interactions so that one person's wishes are not satisfied to the exclusion of all others (dictators excepted).

Thus it comes about naturally that I will sometimes have to do things that I would rather not do, that benefit others rather than me, so that I may gain the other advantages that result from being a member of a society. Actions or results that are agreed to be desirable or 'good' may not necessarily be ones that I would choose myself if I lived in isolation. In fact, Plato believed that the world of objects was only an appearance and that there was an invisible 'reality' in which absolute 'forms' of concepts such as Good and Justice existed and it was this reality that provided the standards by which we should aim to live our lives. When we can do this, we may experience moments in which we gain a glimpse of the reality and a revelatory feeling of understanding. This sounds very much like the 'peak experience' that was described in the twentieth century by Abraham Maslow.

Plato's dialogues cover a variety of topics but all assume the same format, with Socrates engaged in what begins as an almost lighthearted discussion with a friend. The friend will make an apparently straightforward statement about justice, love, or other familiar, if abstract concept and Socrates will respond with some equally simple question of clarification. From there, the debate proceeds with inevitability as Socrates exposes the fact that the other hasn't really considered what he is saying; he may be saying things that are traditionally accepted but, on analysis, they are shown to be mistaken. Continuing then with a series of elucidatory questions, Socrates shows that, in fact, the friend does indeed understand the truth of the situation. The knowledge is actually already there, merely covered over by habitually careless assumptions and ignorance.

Aristotle

Aristotle too, though he denied Plato's 'reality', the invisible world of Forms, argued that the sort of life we ought to pursue if we wish it to be as happy as possible is one which is lived in accordance with reason, which is the most divine element in the human being. This is a recurring theme throughout philosophy and one against which it is difficult to argue. If we do not understand the nature of 'reality', how can we know how to act? We could live our entire lives on the assumption that there is no afterlife for example, seeking self-gratification and ignoring the feelings of others. If this turns out to be wrong we could be reborn as a cockroach or find ourselves burning in hell for the rest of eternity. And that ought to be a cause for concern, since the duration of this life is rather insignificant compared to that of eternity!

Aristotle believed that happiness is the ultimate good, the purpose of human existence. Once we are truly happy, we do not want anything else. The route to happiness lies simply in developing our potentials as far as possible and exercising these within society. He is also responsible for the idea of the 'Golden Mean', so that he believed that the optimum course was that of a balance between excesses. Whatever we do, we should aim for neither extreme of possible courses of action, always using our reason to guide our behavior. To endeavor to keep everything for ourselves is clearly immoral behavior but so, he said, would be to give everything away. If we have a job and a family to look after, we should certainly go to work in order to be able to support them. But we should neither spend all hours slaving away at the office so that we have no time with our children nor neglect our job in order to stay at home.

All virtues operate in this way and form the basis of defining a good and moral person. For example, in response to the emotion of fear, we could train ourselves to be totally oblivious and act without any regard for it – but this would be reckless and foolish. Alternatively, we might be very responsive to it and act very circumspectly – but this would be timid and cowardly.

The correct way to behave is to find the mean between these extremes and that would be courageous.

Cynics

The value of values was called into question by the Cynics, the most famous of whom was Diogenes, a contemporary of Aristotle who lived his later life in a large earthenware container, naked and dirty, 'like a dog' (the literal meaning of the Greek word *cynic*). He derided the ideas of social conventions and national allegiance, for example, as 'false values.' Obviously he had no regard whatsoever for material possessions and instead passionately sought virtue and freedom from desire.

In the face of adversity, there are various ways in which we can respond. If we live in a totalitarian regime we may well be obliged simply to put up with it but in a Western, democratic society, we can usually choose to try to fight it or, as the hippies did in the nineteen-sixties, just 'drop out.'

Theories of ethics, the principles that we use to guide us in our behavior, could be said to arise whenever man is dissatisfied with his own life or the society in which he lives. After all, if we are happy with our lot, why should we want to theorize about it or try to change it? Cynicism came into prominence during the era of Alexander the Great. The effective founder and teacher of Diogenes was Antisthenes, who had been a disciple of Socrates and was no doubt somewhat disturbed following the effective execution of Socrates and the later defeat of Athens by the Spartans. These were troubled times and an obvious way out was simply to denounce the values of society and try to live a life of simple pleasures outside of it. All of the standards of civilization were rejected, from government and private ownership down to marriage and religion. All material possessions were transient and potentially liable to lead to unhappiness. Instead, a life of asceticism was advocated and searching for happiness within oneself.

In essence the philosophy is not different from that of the

traditional monastic life, pursuing virtue and living a frugal existence free from the temptations of a materialistic world. It is of course substantially different from the meaning that is applied to the term 'cynic' today. This change in meaning came about as a result of later people distorting the principles in order to justify their own selfish behavior.

Skeptics

The Skeptics, noting that different peoples had differing opinions on many subjects, wondered how one could ever justify holding a particular belief. Arguments for one view rather than another were usually founded on unproven premises and there seemed to be no means of ever being certain about anything. They concluded long before Kant in the 18th century that we could have no real knowledge about the nature of things and believed that in situations where we are essentially ignorant we ought not to make judgments. This course of action (or perhaps we should call it 'inaction') was thought to lead to peace of mind. The outcome was that adherents behaved in whatever way those around them behaved and did not really believe in anything themselves (what we might now call cynically!). Again, this philosophy offered some consolation to those seeking escape from a difficult life – don't worry about the future since you can never know anything about it anyway. In fact, the above description seems remarkably similar to the way that many of the modern generation seems to behave so that it has clearly lost little of its force as a philosophical outlook on life.

Skepticism was largely of 'academic' interest at the time of its origin. It was taken up by the Academy, the Greek school of philosophy inaugurated by Plato, and the important members of the time would give demonstrations of their skills by arguing points brilliantly one day and then arguing the opposite point of view equally brilliantly the following day. It was superseded by the Epicureans and Stoics in the 3rd century BC but was resurrected in the 16th century AD when it again became dominant. René Descartes attempted to demolish its foundations by returning to basics and showing, step by step, what we could actually be certain about ('I am a thinking thing; therefore I must exist' etc.). In fact he did not succeed ultimately and left skepticism even stronger than it had been before and it later became a key aspect of David Hume's philosophy in the 18th c.

Epicureans

The Epicureans (founded by Epicurus around 300BC) believed that this life was all there was. Matter consists of atoms; there is no 'spiritual' component, no world of 'Forms.' Any 'Gods' are so far away that we can effectively ignore them. Atoms themselves last forever but they are constantly changing their combinations. Our bodies are just one combination, lasting only until we die. We need not fear death because, when it occurs, we will no longer exist to have any concern about it. Our aim therefore in this life should simply be to be happy.

Plato had said that the way we ought to live our lives had nothing to do with pleasure. Aristotle had acknowledged that pleasure was at least a consideration but Epicurus insisted it was all that mattered. Communities were advocated in which pleasures would be sought and, whereas Plato had established the Academy, Epicurus set up the 'Garden.' Here, members existed together in friendship. Moderation was advised (to avoid hangovers!) and people were forbidden to harm others.

The general attitude again rings true for many people today though, needless to say, the ideas are totally rejected by Christianity – no soul, values derived from this life rather than an afterlife and so on. Nowadays, we tend to call this philosophy 'hedonism' and, although we may deep down believe that it is probably the only sensible way to live, we may well frown upon those that we feel openly behave in this manner. In fact, Epicurus himself lived in a manner we would probably regard now as ascetic. He preferred to avoid all excesses and drank water rather than wine, in the belief that those pleasures that resulted in pain were not ultimately pleasures at all, i.e. avoidance of pain was more important than pursuit of pleasure. And it was advised that we should not form close relationships with others because, in the long term, that was likely to lead to unhappiness.

This philosophy thus acknowledged that men do in fact tend to spend their lives in search of pleasure. Perhaps even those who deprive themselves of everyday pleasures and retreat into a monastery are doing it because they want to and perhaps derive some masochistic pleasure from it (cynicism again!). More realistically, it may not be the monastic life in which they are primarily interested but the heavenly rewards that they believe will result from it – i.e. a pleasurable *goal*.

Thus we might go to the gym for exercise, not because we enjoy it per se but because we want the comparatively pleasurable state of being healthy rather than the state of being out of condition and prone to aches and pains. But it was also said that certain pleasures *ought* to be sought because they are intrinsically good, for example friendship, and that some 'excessive' pleasures should be avoided even if they are pleasurable because they lead to pain. Taking drugs or smoking would be an example of the latter. Perhaps modern hedonists tend to ignore this subsidiary advice.

Again, other philosophers, not feeling that the hedonistic outlook on life could possibly be right, soon found fault with it. It did not, for example, address such things as duty. Clearly one has duties to family and society. You could never imagine that it could be 'right' to go out for a drink with your friends rather than attend a school play in which your child was playing a part, even though the former might be thought more pleasurable. When we think about it, we somehow feel that hedonism cannot be right.

Stoics

This is yet another school whose principles still have a ring of truth for the modern age. It began around 300BC, after the fall of Alexander, and lasted until it was superseded by Christianity. Like the Epicureans, they effectively believed that what we see is all that there is but they accepted that nature was governed by rational principles and therefore that reason was the ultimate power.

The 'good life', they claimed, is one lived in accordance with nature. If we feel that we should do one thing rather than another, we can exercise reason to decide whether such an action would be good or bad. Knowing the transience of all things in life (including ourselves) we should not become attached to any of them. By all means enjoy them if you have them, but if you remain unattached, you will not suffer pain and regret if you should lose them. Furthermore, we lose our self-reliance when we become attached to objects – there is the ever-present danger that someone will steal them and then we would lose our equanimity. The things that matter most in life are the ones that cannot be taken away.

If we can genuinely live in this way then we will be as happy as it is possible for us to be. We should accept that things are the way they are and not complain about them or try to change them, indeed without feeling anything about them one way or the other. This is the sort of attitude of grim acceptance and determination that we have come to associate stereotypically with the early industrialized poor, accepting their lot, without complaint, 'stoically.' It is by having desires for things that we cannot obtain that we end up being unhappy, so it is important to try to rid ourselves of them.

$$Happiness = \frac{Possessions}{Desires}$$

The simple formula above explains this very well. If the result is greater than one, you can be said to be generally happy; if less than one generally miserable. Even if you do not have very much, say only the roof over your head and good health, you can still be very happy providing there is nothing that you want. On the other hand, a millionaire with a mansion, Rolls-Royce, swimming pool and film star wife could be really miserable if he wants to be a multimillionaire living on an island without any roads, hates swimming and cannot keep up with his wife's affairs.

The Roman Emperor, Marcus Aurelius, in the 2nd century AD, was essentially stoic in his outlook and his *Meditations* are still widely read today. Typical of this attitude of forbearance, he says for example:

> *When you are outraged by somebody's impudence, ask yourself at once, "Can the world exist without impudent people?" It cannot, so do not ask for impossibilities. That man is simply one of the impudent whose existence is necessary to the world.*

Needless to say, the Stoics were also deterministic in their outlook; they believed that everything happened as it had to happen, according to divine providence, so it was simply stupid to complain about how things were. Some things, such as health and wealth, are clearly more desirable than others, such as sickness and poverty, and we should naturally pursue the former. But if we end up with the latter, it was meant to be, and we should not feel bad about it. Paradoxically, it is through accepting the inevitability of fate that we can be effectively free.

The attitudes of Stoicism seem appropriate if you live in a society in which you are not able to influence your own life. If you cannot improve your lot, then it makes sense to adopt an outlook in which it is still possible to be reasonably happy. In a less oppressive regime where there are opportunities for self-improvement, where the advantages that others possess seem attainable for oneself, it no longer holds the same sort of appeal. Our modern, materialistic, capitalist style society naturally encourages desires for new possessions and a go-get-it mentality.

Plotinus and Neo-Platonism

During the second century AD, Plotinus attempted to revise Plato's concepts relating to the nature of reality in order to incorporate the objections that Aristotle had raised. Most people lived at a level below that at which the intellect was able to comprehend the 'Forms' that Plato had spoken of, the eternal and unchanging basis for the worldly approximations of concepts such as beauty, justice and so on. The highest of the Forms was the 'Good.' From it, the entire universe emanated, becoming increasingly less 'good' as it spread outwards but nevertheless still being 'one thing.' The origin, God if you like, first becomes mind (intellect) and then soul. All things, including ourselves, are souls. The purpose of man was to return to the original state by examining the world and following the good back to its source. It was concepts such as this that greatly influenced Christianity, though the philosophers themselves rejected it because of such notions as salvation through grace. The ideas also had resurgence during the Renaissance, when the writings of Plotinus were translated into Latin.

This is effectively the antithesis of the materialist stance, represented by the Epicureans. We ought to renounce the material world and concern ourselves solely with the 'ideal' world of Forms, aiming to 'become One with' the ultimate Form of the Good. The everyday world is primarily one of hardship and misery (or at least was so in the time of Plotinus) and, if we are to search for happiness, we must do so by reflection and imagination, not through the senses. This was, of course, a very 'anti-scientific' view (though science as we know it did not then exist of course), encouraging us to look within for meaning to our lives rather than pursuing external goals.

Early Christianity

St. Augustine was one of the major early proponents of Christianity, being a bishop in what is now Algeria for the second half of his life. In addition to Plato and Plotinus, he was also influenced by Manichaeism, the idea of the Persian Mani that the universe consisted of twin powers of 'Good/Light/Spirit' and 'Evil/Darkness/Matter' and that this was represented in man by the soul striving to free itself from the body.

Augustine's thoughts on such things as the nature of time and mind anticipated the much later philosophers Kant and Descartes. He claimed that God was outside of time, having created it with the universe. There is only the present, with the future consisting only of present expectations and the past being present memories. We know that we are and that we think but not where we came from or what our precise nature might be.

In his autobiography, he confesses how he was obsessed by sex in his youth, famously praying, "Give me chastity and continence, only not yet," and being granted his wish by the time that he eventually got married! He believed that lust was effectively a punishment for the fall of Adam, its feeling of shamefulness resulting from the fact that it operates regardless of our will. It seems inevitable that much of the guilt associated with anything to do with sex results from ideas such as this, which have been propagated in the name of religion. It certainly seems strange that it should have been thought desirable that something we so much associate with pleasure ought to be divorced from it; that sex should ideally be simply a necessary and quite unemotional act for the purpose of begetting children. Since Darwin, it has been quite apparent that the sex drive and its associated rapture play a vital role in the purely mechanistic propagation of the species and the genetic predisposition for this to continue is inevitable.

The Manicheans stated that man's soul was divine and that it was only the body that was evil. To the extent that we identified with the soul, this meant that we could abdicate responsibility for evil actions, effectively claiming that they were the body's fault. Although initially going along with this, Augustine later revised his position to one that claimed the evil in the world was our doing and not a preexisting condition of the universe or something imposed by God. But he agreed that the soul is essentially what we are and is immortal.

It is not obvious whether he believed that our souls were also created or somehow always existed or what the ultimate purpose of all this might be but, as far as this life is concerned, our aim should be to shun the limited and temporary world of the senses, which we normally regard as being all that there is, and strive instead to attain to the eternal realm of spirit, truth and goodness. He came to believe, however, that, though it was possible to improve our soul in this way, it could be done only through the grace of God.

This was contrary to the claims of another ecclesiastical philosopher of the time, the Welshman Morgan, who for some reason was known as Pelagius, the Greek equivalent of the name (meaning 'man of the sea'). He argued that man could *himself* choose to act virtuously, so that he could eventually go to heaven as a result of his own efforts. This went against the doctrine of original sin and caused great contention amongst his contemporaries. It is still known today as the 'Pelagian Controversy.' Augustine eventually had him declared a heretic.

The orthodox view was that, once Adam had eaten from the forbidden apple, he and Eve lost their free will and ability to abstain from sin and this penalty has been passed on to everyone else ever since. Only by being baptized into the Christian faith can this be redeemed (through God's grace) so that we avoid going to hell.

Following the death of Augustine (not that this was the trigger!), the Western world descended into the 'Dark Ages', which lasted until the end of the tenth century, with bloody wars and little time for philosophizing. Barbarians, Vandals and Attila the Hun are just a few evocative names from this period. The church seems to have been the sole (soul) repository of serious thinking – outside the church most people were illiterate – but most of their efforts were devoted to converting the invaders.

One of the few philosophers worthy of note in passing was the Roman Boethius, who lived at the end of the fifth and early sixth century and wrote a book appropriately titled *The Consolation of Philosophy* (while he was in prison awaiting execution). He was still principally influenced by Plato and Aristotle, as much of Western philosophy has been ever since. He affirmed that happiness came from 'good', not pleasure, equating 'blessedness' with God – those who become truly happy achieve divinity, in effect become God.

John the Scot was an Irishman! (This was the meaning of 'Scotus.') He taught at the court of the French king in the ninth century. He had a number of heretical beliefs but managed to escape persecution. He believed, for example, that truth could be derived by reason and not just by divine revelation; in fact, in the event of any discrepancy, he preferred the former. He divided Nature into four classes. The first was God, who is uncreated but creates. The second equates to Plato's realm of Forms, that which is created and also creates, the essence of all things. The third is created but does not create; it contains the entire perceivable universe. The fourth neither creates nor is created; it is the end of all, God (again). God, not being objective in any sense, is unknowable, even to Himself. Everything comes from God and returns to Him; is not in any real sense ever distinct from Him – this is the theory of Pantheism. Sin results when man turns away from God towards himself.

Much of the wisdom that had been cultivated by the Greeks died out in the West during the Dark Ages. Fortunately it was kept alive in the East and ideas and writings were effectively reintroduced in the twelfth century. One of the key philosophers responsible for this was Averroes. He lived in Cordoba in Spain and was Islamic, better known as Ibn Rushd. His work was later translated into Latin and became very influential in Europe, though he was effectively only commenting upon Aristotle.

He believed that it was the duty of the philosopher to examine religious beliefs and 'divine revelation' in order to discover the truth and he wrote a book, *Incoherence of the Incoherence*, to argue this. He maintained, for example, that the human soul is not immortal but that the intellect is; this, however, being universal and not individual. There is only one truth, determined through philosophical enquiry and then simply followed via religious laws. Acting in accordance with this would inevitably maximize happiness. It is interesting that he believed that the capacity for happiness was proportionate to one's intellectual abilities. This related to the extent to which a person is able to 'know' God.

The reintroduction of Aristotle's philosophy was bound to affect thinking significantly. The earlier philosophers had been principally influenced by Plato and the Neo-Platonists but St. Thomas Aquinas based his thoughts upon Aristotle and was responsible for making considerable changes to the attitudes of the church in the thirteenth century. His ideas (called 'Thomism') became the foundation of the Catholic Church and remain significant today. Whereas the emphasis had previously been upon religious dogma and faith, he now emphasized the importance of the intellect and reason acting upon observation. With Aristotle having laid the foundations for what might be called a scientific attitude, this paved the way towards the idea that knowledge derives from experience. Called 'empiricism', this belief was more clearly expressed by William of Ockham in the next century, though it was not fully developed until much later in the seventeenth century England of Francis Bacon and John Locke.

Aquinas acknowledged that revelation is the optimum method for realizing God but also insisted that it was possible to use reason and he was responsible for producing five 'proofs' of the existence of God. As far as happiness is concerned, he claimed that it was man's nature to seek it and we could not help doing so. But it is not to be gained through sensory means and is not dependent upon pleasures of the body, mind or intellect. The most happiness that we can achieve in this life is from contemplation of God but this is a limited form only and only in heaven can we achieve true joy in meeting with God.

William of Ockham is best known for the so-called 'Ockham's Razor.' This was the principle that, in the absence of any more specific guiding knowledge, the simplest explanation for any given phenomenon should be assumed to be the correct one. This is often summed up these days by the acronym KISS – keep it simple, stupid! He maintained that we should use observation, followed by reason in order to make sense of the world; mere argument or speculation was insufficient. In this respect he could be seen as the first advocate of what we might now call the 'scientific method.' He also predated the 18th century philosopher David Hume in recognizing that, when we say that A *causes* B, what we are really saying is that, on all of the occasions that we observed B, it had been preceded by A. But B does not *necessarily* follow A; it only happens to have done so when we observed it and might not next time. Things happen because God wills them to do so and He might will things differently next time.

Science

The age of increasing importance of science is usually claimed to have begun with Copernicus in the early 16th century when he argued that the sun is the center of the solar system and not the earth as the church had always insisted. (This is stated in the Psalms of the Old Testament and by the Greek astronomer Ptolemy in the 2nd century.) In fact, so afraid was Copernicus of incurring the wrath of the clergy that publication of his beliefs did not take place until after his death. Even Galileo, later confirming the facts by telescope, was forced to deny it since he wished to stay alive. Galileo advocated that all prior beliefs and opinion should be kept out of scientific observation, which should be completely objective. Needless to say, once such ideas gained support, the authority of the church began to diminish and their dogmatic pronouncements about the nature of everything began to be supplanted by more tentative suggestions based upon specific observation and experiment.

Isaac Newton was born in the same year that Galileo died and his discoveries were to have a devastating effect on religious faith. Once it became accepted that the workings of the universe could be understood through scientific laws, the idea of a divine creation became suspect. Man was just a tiny phenomenon in a vast universe, no longer the center of everything. This had a profound effect upon man's self-image and outlook. Previously it had been believed that our earth was effectively *the* creation and that man was the most important being in it, capable of communing with God and aspiring to union with Him. Henceforth it became increasingly apparent that the earth was insignificant in the immensity of the universe and the concomitant conclusion was that man himself was nowhere near as important as had previously been supposed.

And, if everything moved according to principles of action and reaction, gravitation and so on, in an essentially mechanistic way, what did this imply for man's free will and morality? If you could know the initial conditions and the forces that acted upon a particular body, then the outcome was inevitable. What place could God have in all of this? Henceforth, people would look to science to provide explanations for the phenomena that they saw around them rather than accepting what the bishops or rabbis told them was the case.

The advent of science marked the boundary between the old world and the modern. It did not, however, open the way towards any understanding of self or purpose or make us more satisfied with what we had. In fact, it led towards materialism and an ever-increasing concentration on detail. Instead of looking inwards, the world of objectivity was suddenly opened up in ways that had previously been unimaginable. It was now possible to continue to find out more and more about less and less, as someone once cynically pointed out until, in the limit, we would know everything about nothing. Discoveries and inventions have diverted us ever since, making life easier and perhaps more enjoyable but doing little to explain to us what exactly it is really about. Where would we be without the automobile, refrigerator, television and the atomic bomb? How would we survive if we couldn't look forward to holidays in the Bahamas and choosing the sex of our future children?

At least the scientific method developed by Francis Bacon at the end of the 16th century gave us the tools to enable us to question our beliefs and approach new ideas more circumspectly. He advocated looking for patterns in repeated, controlled experiments, putting forward hypotheses to explain our observations and devising new experiments to test them – ideas familiar to all of us today; clearly valuable if we are trying to understand the world 'out there' in an objective manner.

He pointed out that we have an innate tendency to accept what our senses tell us and we are far too easily persuaded by opinion, whether our own or those of someone else. Existing systems, philosophical or religious, as well as language itself, can also deceive us. We need to be on our guard against all of these things. Bacon is also remembered for stating that "knowledge is power." But is it happiness or fulfillment? And, as we may ask shortly, in the light of philosophers such as Bishop George Berkeley, what does it actually mean to know all these facts about 'objects'?

This is not to say that Bacon was an atheist. On the contrary, like Averroes he believed that it was possible to discover truths from divine revelation as well as through reason. Faith, indeed, could triumph over reason in such matters. Apparently he rejected the Copernican theory for example, continuing to believe that the sun orbited the earth. In fact, science was never going to be of any help in investigating the nature of spiritual matters and of limited value in respect of subjects such as consciousness and happiness.

The nature of the scientific method was inevitably going to tend towards a materialistic view of life, with potentially everything being ultimately analyzable. A contemporary of Galileo and secretary of Bacon, Thomas Hobbes stated this view most clearly, believing that everything, including ourselves, is effectively a machine. Hobbes believed that our desires are driven automatically by mental needs that can never be satisfied and we vainly attempt to avoid the inevitability of death. Our natural instinct is always to act in our own self-interest, regardless of others and we have to strive to subdue this in order to gain the benefits of security etc. that result from living in society with others. He is famous for his quotation that, without these benefits, life would be "solitary, poor, nasty, brutish and short." Accordingly, his political philosophy advocates an absolute ruler for his ideal society which, although simply a compromise, would at least ensure peace – far preferable to the anarchy that would result if man was left to his own devices. Needless to say, his books were banned by the church.

Hobbes had very straightforward notions of some of the issues dealt with here. Things were said to be good if we desire or love them and bad if we have an aversion to or hate them – there simply are no absolutes. Everything is mechanical and the idea of free will a logical absurdity. Religion was simply approved superstition resulting from the fear of invisible forces.

The scientific method has great appeal to the ego. It gives us a sense of somehow being in control. We observe something that we do not fully understand and investigate and theorize in a way that it is fully consistent with our existing knowledge and experience. We set up tests to see what happens in novel situations and modify our understanding accordingly. We put forward possible explanations for the observed behavior and use these to predict what might happen under conditions that we have not yet witnessed. If the predictions are correct then we have an explanation that is satisfying to our intellect. This differs radically from the so-called explanations of religion, where we are asked to believe in totally illogical events supposedly engineered by a God of whom we can never have any objective knowledge.

Mathematics is an even more logical and self-consistent system. It begins with premises that are intuitively obvious, such as that a straight line is the shortest distance between two points, and proceeds by a series of logically unarguable steps to conclusions that may seem quite novel and unintuitive. Descartes was a mathematician and he wanted to apply this sort of process to his own experience. He realized that our senses are often fooled and are therefore unreliable. We have dreams that we believe to be real at the time. How do we know that all our experiences are not being input electronically to our brain, itself isolated in a vat by a malevolent demon?

He reasoned that, even if this were true, we could still be sure of one thing, namely that 'I' am some sort of being that is having these experiences, however delusional – i.e. I exist. From this starting point, he went on to reason that he was a mind. It is only by virtue of 'thinking' that I know I exist, where 'thinking' includes imagining, feeling etc. Once thinking ceases, there is no longer any evidence. (Clearly he was completely unaware of the practice of meditation in its modern sense – anyone who has experienced the depths of meditation, totally without thoughts, will know the pure awareness of 'I.') He maintained that all conclusions reached simply through logical and rational steps, without the benefit of the senses, must also be true.

This power of the faculty of reason (Rationalism) and the

importance of knowledge (Epistemology) became the two most important elements of philosophical endeavor for the next few hundred years and entrenched the scientific method even more firmly than before. Ironically, part of Descartes' process of reasoning from the certainty of his own existence to the objective truths of science involved the proof of the existence of God. The very reasoning power that he was using, he claimed, came from God. He also went on to argue for example that, since God was good, he could not be deceitful therefore objects must exist because they appear to do so. He recognized that the evidence for 'things' came from thoughts and perceptions *in our mind*, rather than externally, and this was very important for subsequent philosophers. He also assumed that thoughts need a *thinker*, which does not go without saying.

It is worth mentioning in passing the observation of a contemporary of Descartes, Blaise Pascal, on belief in God – the so-called 'Wager' analogy. He noted that, if we have doubts as to whether or not God exists, it must be to our advantage to wager that He does. In this case, if it turns out that we are correct, we will be rewarded eternally in heaven and will have the advantage of the consoling thoughts of this during our lifetime. If it turns out that He doesn't exist, obviously we will not go to heaven but then we will be dead anyway so it will not make much difference. On the other hand, if we decide not to believe in God when He really does exist, we will suffer everlasting torment in hell and have only the minor advantage in our lifetime of not having to read the Bible or go to church.

Descartes and the mind-body problem

Descartes' separation of man into the two aspects of mind and matter became the principal way in which Westerners subsequently viewed the world. Matter is extended in space, can be divided and so on, while mind is indivisible and seems to exist separate from the body, somehow outside of space. This is the theory known as Cartesian Dualism. Unfortunately, he was never able to explain how such completely different 'substances' were able to interact. The idea of an immaterial 'little me' somehow sitting in the brain (Descartes thought the soul resided in the pineal gland) and interpreting the information transmitted from the eyes and other material senses just did not make sense. How could this interface work? The so-called 'mind-body problem' has intrigued philosophers ever since and no universally accepted model of the nature of the self has yet emerged.

One of his disciples, a Dutchman called Arnold Geulincx, suggested that the mind and body were separately governed by God, who kept the two in synchronization, like clocks. Thus, when we decide to do something and it happens, such as getting out of bed, there is no actual interaction between the two, no 'willing' as such, it is simply the consequence of the two being synchronized. A similar theory, called Occasionalism, was proposed by the French priest, Nicolas Malebranche. He said that neither mental nor physical events *cause* other events. Instead, what we call a cause is simply the *occasion* for God to exercise his will and instigate what we call the effect; there is no actual connection between the two events at all. All of this meant that life is strictly deterministic, with no place for free will and everything happening according to divine law.

Malebranche also disagreed with Descartes' claimed awareness by the mind of its own nature as a 'thinking thing.' He thought that all that we could know objectively was that there was some sort of conscious activity; we could never actually know anything about the essential nature of the self that was doing the thinking – we can know *that* we are but not *what* we are. Furthermore, he said that our senses are unreliable for telling us anything about the true nature of things.

Leibniz

Yet another variation was proposed by the philosopher Gottfried

Leibniz, who was also an important geologist, mathematician and physicist. The book *Candide* by Voltaire satirized Leibniz in the character of Dr. Pangloss for his proclaimed belief that God had created the "best of all possible worlds." Since God is perfect, he argued, he would naturally do this. A world in which there is free will is bound to contain some evil but this must be better than a supposedly 'good' one that did not allow free will.

Leibniz thought that everything, mental or physical, was effectively a separate entity, which he called a *monad*, which could not be affected by any other entity. He said that some monads were 'in harmony' with others so that when an event occurs in one, for example an alarm clock going off, a harmonious event (or not) occurs in another, i.e. I am awoken by a ringing sound. It is not that the alarm wakes me up – the two events are not causally connected – but that there is a pre-established harmony between the monads. These monads are not 'matter', whose existence he denied, but effectively 'souls.' 'I' am made up of innumerable of these things, though there is one dominant one, the mind, to which all of the others are subservient.

In effect, what Leibniz was saying was that everything does happen for a reason – there are no 'accidents' – but we cannot always know what those reasons are. Possibly reassuring, but then again is this really saying anything useful? Most modern scientists believe that everything will ultimately be explicable but, for the time being, the world can often seem to be a very chaotic place. And, while there remain so many unanswered questions, it will always be plausible to assert that many of them are unanswerable.

Leibniz was the inventor of mathematical logic, which is made up of statements that can be analyzed to determine whether they are true or false. This is in contrast with statements about the world, where we have to examine the facts to which they relate in order to find out whether they are true or not. Truths of reason are 'necessary' and it would be self-contradictory to deny them, whereas truths of fact are 'contingent', they just happen to be so and might easily be otherwise. Much of the philosophy following Leibniz hinged on these observations. He was also responsible for formalizing the proofs for the existence of God that had been spoken of at various times by earlier philosophers such as Aristotle and Descartes. These were later discredited by Kant.

Hobbes was one of a number of philosophers who simply concluded that Descartes' initial separation of mind and body was wrong. He thought that so-called mental events were actually only combinations of matter in motion. The movement of matter in the brain, for example, actually *is* what we call 'thoughts.' This laid the foundation for the reemergence of materialism in the eighteenth century, a theory which gained more and more prominence as science 'explained' the functioning of the nervous system and perceptions etc. But it did not explain how the movement of chemicals around the bloodstream and electrical impulses in the brain could somehow appear in consciousness as the color yellow or as the memory of a day by the seaside. A surgeon probing into the brain of a conscious patient would not find any pear drops even though the patient might smell them.

Spinoza

Benedict Spinoza was the first major philosopher to tackle the problem of a lack of free will in the then-current thinking. Its consequence was a lack of moral choice, and he did not see where God might fit into such a scheme. He argued that God cannot be limited in any way since He is perfect and infinite. There cannot be anything that is not God. Therefore God must be both mind and matter; individual souls and objects are simply aspects of God. It is then acceptable that there is no such thing as free will because everything that happens is part of God's nature and could not be otherwise. Some things may appear evil to us but this is only because we are seeing them from our limited perspective. He recognized that we are driven by self-interest but believed that, once we realize that we are part of a single whole and not separate creatures, our behavior will change. We will then act wisely, and will be happy even in the face of apparent adversity.

And this much seems logically reasonable: if we could be convinced that we are not isolated individuals, separate minds locked in discrete bodies but somehow one and the same, in a world that only appears to be distinct and hostile, then our attitudes might indeed be changed. Perhaps we do only behave selfishly and 'wrongly' because of an erroneous belief in our own separately motivated ego and, as a result, end up miserable and dissatisfied with life.

Spinoza also regarded time as being essentially unreal. (Kant later argued that time is merely a tool that the mind uses to try to make sense of 'reality', about which we can never have any objective knowledge.) If this is accepted then it does not make any sense to worry about the 'past' or 'future' – viewed from the perspective of God, all is timeless. This view also meant that any idea of living a 'good' life with the intention of going to a 'heaven' after death was quite erroneous. Needless to say, this did not go down too well with the authorities and he was excommunicated from the Jewish faith and cursed with all of the curses in the book of the Law. Other Jews were forbidden to go within six feet of him and Christians simply regarded him as an atheist. (As will be realized by now, being a philosopher is often no joke!)

According to Spinoza, the idea of the world or our own life 'getting better' is meaningless. The amount of good and bad in total remains the same. We, too, should endeavor to see the world in this way, *sub specie æternitatis*, as he called it – under the aspect of eternity. And it is no use arguing that we can prevent future eventualities if we do something about them now for, as already pointed out, Spinoza believed that things would happen regardless – we are powerless to change anything. Once we understand all of this, we will no longer act out of desire or fear because we will know the futility of wishing things to be other than as they are. Full intellectual understanding of all of this, which Spinoza called 'love of God', should be the ultimate aim of our lives.

Spinoza was one of the philosophers who specifically set out to discover whether there is anything that, once found or obtained, will provide continuous and supreme happiness. He acknowledged the traditional sources as being rich, famous and experiencing pleasures of the senses and conceded the danger of abandoning those pursuits and looking elsewhere. But he found that it was necessary to do so because the customary pursuits required so much energy that there was none left over for looking elsewhere – all are intensely absorbing.

In the case of pleasure, once it is satisfied, it is usually followed by misery and dulling of the mind so that, again, we are unable to think of anything else. With riches and fame, the more we achieve, the more we seem to want so that, again, our energy is tied up in the search. Riches frequently lead to envy of others, theft and even death. And modern status seekers in the workplace are well aware of the effort involved in seeking promotion, the backbiting and other devious skills that are involved. Overindulgence in physical pleasures leads to ill health and early death. Obviously the supposed 'good' of these common pursuits entail clear 'evils.' Accordingly, he decided to abandon them and search for his 'certain good.'

Locke and Empiricism

Born some eighteen years before the death of Descartes, the Englishman John Locke claimed that reason was *not* the principal means for finding out about the world, as the earlier philosopher had contended. Instead, he advocated an empirical approach to knowledge, i.e. using one's senses to actually see what the case is. This is the only means for obtaining raw data and we use reason subsequently to make sense of it. Only then can it become knowledge. He believed his own purpose in life was to enquire into human knowledge to discover its limits and the extent to which we could be certain of it.

Unlike modern, evolutionary psychologists, he believed that we are effectively born with no innate knowledge, a metaphorical 'blank slate.' All of our knowledge and understanding is therefore built upon information derived from our senses. Everything we know or think about ultimately comes from experience. The limits of what we can know about reality are fixed by the abilities of the senses and the associated mental equipment.

There is a danger of wondering what all of this has to do with the meaning of our lives. Is it not all simply airy imaginings, arguing about concepts that have little relevance in our everyday world? Well, no. If we are wondering what we ought to do, we are bound to ask ourselves what reasons there might be for acting in one way rather than another. Any grounds for such reasons must come from our existing knowledge about the world and our place in it. This knowledge can only arise from a few sources. The main ones are by reasoning from a more basic set of premises (which is what Descartes was doing) or by observing the world and drawing conclusions or making inferences in a broadly scientific way (which is what empiricism proposes). Therefore we do need to be aware of this and decide for ourselves how trustworthy the data might be, even if we do not actually make any significant investigation into them.

Locke believed that external objects had what he called 'primary' qualities, which were aspects that could be measured scientifically such as length, mass, velocity and so on. Those aspects such as smell and taste, he called 'secondary' qualities, and he said that these were not 'intrinsic' to the object itself (they could not be measured scientifically) but were simply a subjective interpretation in our mind, triggered by the primary qualities.

He said that we can only ever be aware of these *qualities*, which are effectively transactions between an actual object and ourselves as the subject; we cannot know anything about the matter itself independent of these characteristics nor of ourselves independent of these experiences. Most importantly, the conclusions of this approach meant that we can never know any absolute truths about the universe, only develop possible hypotheses that seem to explain our observations. Once we accept this, we can stop wasting our time trying to understand things that are forever beyond our ken.

He recognized several varieties of knowledge. The most certain type of knowledge that we have is 'intuitive', as in the certainty with which we know that 2+2=4. We may not be able to say how we know this to be true but we have no doubt about it. Sometimes, we can see the truth about something by reasoning from something that is intuitively obvious via several steps, each of which, in turn, is also intuitively obvious. In this way we can arrive, by what he called 'demonstration', at some new knowledge that we did not have to begin with. This knowledge is almost as certain as the first, though we might make a mistake in the reasoning process.

A third type is that which arrives via our senses, 'sensitive' knowledge, which has a quality about it that is different from something that is simply remembered or dreamt. The smell of a flower, for example, may be brought to mind but is so much more immediate and positive when we actually go out into the garden and put our nose to the flower. Here, however, we know that the senses can be mistaken, as in an optical illusion, so that the knowledge is less certain. But in general the difference in quality between actual sense and remembrance of it gives us a high degree of confidence of the existence of external objects.

With these three types of knowledge, then, we discover that we can be directly certain of only one thing, namely our own existence – to this extent he agreed with Descartes. Beyond this, we could demonstrate, he thought, the existence of God. But as regards everything else, we could only know those things about which we could derive sensitive knowledge. If they were not accessible to our senses, then we couldn't find out anything about them at all and could not even be sure of their existence.

As regards how we ought to act, Locke believed that the aim of all our desires is to achieve happiness, which is effectively the ultimate pleasure. Things are 'good' to the extent that they bring about pleasure or minimize pain. But, believing in God as he did, he also insisted that we should exercise control over our desires so as to live a virtuous life – breaking the commandments would lead us to hell. God has provided us with senses for acquiring data and from these we derive beliefs and He has given us the faculty of reason in order to be able to turn this into knowledge.

The idea of using reason to validate the moral instructions of the Bible did not go down very well with many of his contemporaries, who thought this tantamount to encouraging atheism. They also preferred to think that the basic principles of morality were somehow innate rather than instilled into us during childhood.

Berkeley and Idealism

Bishop George Berkeley in particular objected to Locke's classification of qualities into primary and secondary. This suggested that our senses were unreliable; that reality was one thing while our senses told us something else. Such ideas could only lead us into doubt and skepticism. If the ordinary person saw that philosophers, who had devoted their lives to studying the nature of knowledge and reality, were coming up with ideas that were contradictory to all of their experience and common sense, it could only lead to atheism.

He showed that, if we accepted the empiricist view that all of our knowledge derives from experience, then we are inevitably led to deny any objective reality to the world. We can only ever know anything via our senses. Locke had said that there were real objects possessing primary qualities but Berkeley argued that our awareness of the primary is really no different from our awareness of the secondary qualities. We are only aware of form, size and motion and so on as a result of sight and touch, and these are ultimately only perceptions in our minds just the same.

That this is all subjective can be shown by the fact that our interpretation depends upon where we are and what we are doing at the time. We can easily misjudge the size of something if there is no known object in the vicinity with which to compare it. If we ourselves are moving, we can mistake the degree to which another object is moving. Everything about a supposed external object is in fact in our mind and there can never be any independent validation that it exists other than when we are aware of it.

It is pointless trying to argue that an object has certain qualities that we cannot perceive and that these are the cause of our perceptions since, by definition, this could never be proven. Furthermore, it would not make any sense to say that our ideas and impressions are *like* the supposed real object because we are attempting to claim that the object exists relatively unchanging over time, whereas our thoughts are transient and change frequently. Our sensations are *like* sensations, which only exist within living things. We cannot even imagine something, with qualities other than those that we perceive, existing alone without someone to perceive them. As soon as we imagine it, it is by definition an idea in our minds. And if qualities that we cannot perceive did exist, again by definition, we could never be aware of them.

Berkeley argued that all of this followed from the Empiricist assumption that all of our knowledge derives from experience. Since that experience itself comes from sense data alone and all these consist of ideas in mind, we can only ever experience ideas and never any 'real objects.' Everything that we perceive is an idea and ideas cannot exist outside of the mind. (This includes the brain itself, so that the brain is in the mind, not vice versa!) As he famously put it, "to be is to be perceived."

But he did not claim that the contents of a room disappeared when he left it (nor that we disappear when we are in deep sleep). He also acknowledged that he was not able to dictate how particular objects appeared, as one might expect to be able to do if they existed entirely within one's own mind. He believed that objects appear to continue to exist independently of any specific observer because the 'ideas' actually exist in the mind of God.

Thus his claim was that there are only two elements to our perceptual experience: the perceiver and the ideas in mind that he perceives. There are no such things as 'material objects.' This theory was called Immaterialism or Idealism (nothing to do with the pursuit of ideals but the theory that what is real is effectively contained within our minds or ideas). Needless to say, most people find his claims fantastical to say the least, despite the fact that they are unable to find any obvious counter arguments. In fact, at the time, Berkeley believed his theory corresponded most clearly with common sense and said that it was held alike by ordinary men (the 'vulgar') and philosophers.

In fact, so-called objects in dreams seem perfectly real while we are still in the dream; it is only after we wake up that we feel them somehow to be different. Furthermore this difference is not based upon the belief that dream objects are 'only in our minds' whereas waking objects consist of *matter*. In fact, our perception of the relative reality of waking objects is based upon such things as their seeming duration in place and time. E.g. the table that was in the room next door will almost certainly still be there the next time that we go into the room in the waking state but quite likely will not if it is a dream. Also, in the waking state, objects tend to remain the same, whereas in a dream a table might well change into a rhinoceros before our very dream eyes. Finally, the amount of control that we can exert over objects differs. E.g. we may be able to throw the dream table/rhinoceros into orbit or be unable to budge it at all whereas the waking table will usually behave in a predictable fashion. (In Advaita, the 7th century philosopher Gaudapada addresses all these objections and concludes that the waking and dream states are equally unreal. This is dealt with in detail in my book *A-U-M: Awakening to Reality*.)

We do not typically use the idea of matter at all when we identify an object as real or imaginary. Matter is simply a rationalization after the fact of the observed behavior and is not necessarily a useful concept. And, of course, we can never see 'matter', we only experience different physical properties.

Hume and Skepticism

The Scottish philosopher David Hume accepted Locke's empiricism and also agreed with Berkeley that we cannot ever know that there is a world outside of and separate from ourselves. Indeed he claimed not to understand what people meant by the idea of 'substance.' We only know about perceptions, color, sound, taste and so on. If this thing called 'substance' is something else, we have no knowledge of it – why invent it? If we took away the sensible qualities of things there would be nothing left, would there? Why should we need anything to explain or support our perceptions and impressions? Questions about why they arise are unnecessary and the answers suggested to explain them are unintelligible. The idea of 'mind' is just as illogical. If we simply dropped both of them, we would have no need to try to imagine ways in which such supposedly different 'things' might interact, as Descartes had wasted so much of his time doing.

He was also skeptical of Descartes' conviction of his own existence as a thinking individual and made his own attempts to find some irreducible 'self' of which he could be certain. He decided that whenever he attempted to look for 'himself' he could only find thoughts, feelings and perceptions; never a 'self' that is the perceiver, feeler and thinker. And so he concluded that there was no such thing. One feels one wants to get hold of him and shake him and say: "Yes, when you look, all that you find *are* thoughts, feelings and perceptions but *who is it* who finds this? What is the 'who' that is doing the looking?" He also felt similarly about God. We may well feel convinced that there is a God – this is effectively the definition of faith, a firm conviction without any empirical evidence – but this is not the same as knowledge.

There are really only two useful types of thought according to Hume. Reasoning based upon mathematical concepts is based upon ideas that can be known intuitively to be true and they do not rely upon any external beliefs. Direct impressions that arise from observation and can be tested through experience are the other type. Anything else is ultimately irrelevant because it can never be validated. He famously said that any books dealing with other things (amongst which we must include the Bible, for example) should be 'committed to the flames', "for it can contain nothing but sophistry and illusion." The quotation about the metaphysician's black cat given earlier could have been made by Hume.

In fact he was scathing about the pursuits of metaphysicians who deceived themselves with their inventions of clever explanations for things that could never be explained, thinking that the terms which they had devised were actually significant and intelligible. He thought that poets and children could be excused such flights of imagination but not supposedly intelligent philosophers. We cannot directly experience, define, investigate or test the things about which we are asking questions. How can we hope to find valid answers and how would we know if we did? Still, if we find it amusing…

Hume also had strong, counterintuitive views upon the subject of causality. We take it for granted in our day-today life that some things *cause* other things. Indeed this is so fundamental that we rarely give it any thought. We put water in the kettle for our cup of coffee in the morning and flick a switch. Unless there has been a power cut, we simply know that, in a couple of minutes, the water will come to the boil. Electricity flowing through the heating element causes the water to heat up. But Hume pointed out that we do not ever see something called 'causality.' All that we are aware of is that, in all of the situations that we have encountered previously, one thing has been followed by another. We have not experienced a situation in which, for example, the kettle did not come to the boil after switching on – unless the fuse in the plug had blown or the lead had come loose etc., i.e. unless there was some other condition to explain why, thus constituting a different 'cause' for the failure.

All that we can say is that B has always followed A in our experience. But our experience has been minimal in terms of the infinite universe and it is a gross assumption to think that B will continue to follow A for the rest of eternity. Also, our understanding is limited. We might, for example, once have claimed that day 'causes' night. After all, night has always followed day in our experience. But we now know that these are both inevitable consequences of the earth's rotation as it moves around the sun so that the notion of cause and effect between the two does not apply.

In the case of the kettle above, we might also believe that we know that, if we switch it on and raise the temperature of the water to 100°C, then the water will boil. However, if this is done at the top of a mountain, where the air pressure is much lower, it will (usually!) be found that it will boil quite a few degrees lower than this. Conversely, if heated in a pressure cooker, for example, the water will not boil at all at 100°C. In fact, it has only been observed to boil at precisely 100°C under normal atmospheric pressure. But Hume maintained that there can be no evidence that this will happen next time. We might find that it boils as soon as we switch it on, even though the water has just come out of the cold tap, or we might find that it will not boil at all. Either of these eventualities would pose some interesting problems for Physics but that is not the point.

When it comes to our own desires and actions, we assume that if we want Y, then we have to do X. Of course many things can go wrong in human affairs, which tend to be more complex than boiling water, but nevertheless we rely on causality. Without it, motivation and purposeful action would be meaningless. In fact, we rely on habit. What has happened before in our interactions with things will happen again. We discover that fire burns when we are children and periodically reinforce this throughout our lives. The two things have been experienced as going together and the related ideas are connected in our minds. But, if we think that we want to get up when the alarm clock rings in the morning and then later find that we are washing ourselves in the bathroom, we may say that we 'decided' to get up and that *this* was the cause of our getting up. In fact, myriad things have occurred in this process, involving electrochemical reactions in the brain, hormones in the blood, oxygen absorption in the lungs and thousands more, most of which we would not claim to be able to control. It also involves the thorny question of free will, on which there is a separate section below.

We cannot help but believe in things, external and internal, and in causes and effects between them but we do so only through habit and because it is easy and convenient to do so. Rationally, we have no justification for any of these beliefs. This is the extreme position of skepticism at which Hume arrived. It also followed that there is no point in studying philosophy except in so far as it is an interesting way of passing the time. All our actions are ultimately irrational since they can never be based upon any real knowledge. The reaction to these claims from contemporary philosophers was not to refute them but to resort to faith and emotion, effectively arguing that the heart outranked the mind on such matters. His demonstration of the unreasonableness of the empirical method led to the growth of 'unreason' as a reaction.

Rousseau and Revolution

The reaction to the perceived unreasonableness of the empirical method was most apparent in the philosophy of Rousseau in France, which eventually contributed to the Romantic Movement, with its disdain for reason and advocacy of giving free rein to feelings and instinct. It was also taken up by those who instigated the French Revolution. Rousseau believed that man is inherently good but that the rise of civilization, begun through the inequalities created in claiming 'private property', had corrupted us. Voltaire, on reading of his ideas, sarcastically commented that he was too old to start walking on all fours or searching out the savages in Canada. They also quarreled over an earthquake in Lisbon. Voltaire saw in it a justification for questioning the beneficence of a God that would allow such a thing. Rousseau thought it served them right for living in seven-story houses rather than out in the countryside where they ought to have been. In any case, he did not think that we could use reason when talking about God; our attitude should be one of awe and reverence.

More dangerously, Rousseau was advocating democracy in his writings and questioning the divine right of kings. He believed that there should be discussion and agreement amongst the people to determine what he called the "general will." This would then be formed into legislation which, once accepted by everyone, would be forcibly imposed. His best-known work, *The Social Contract*, opens with the challenging statement: *"Man is born free, and everywhere he is in chains. One man thinks himself the master of others, but remains more of a slave than they are."*

His ideas represent the precursors of totalitarian ideologies such as Communism and Fascism. The immediate consequence of his philosophy was the 'Reign of Terror' instigated by Robespierre, whose quotations reflect the ideals of Rousseau:

I am no courtesan, nor moderator, nor Tribune, nor defender of the people: I am myself the people.

The general will rules in society as the private will governs each separate individual.

One single will is necessary.

Kant and Transcendental Idealism

Several of the beliefs of Immanuel Kant struck a chord with my own thinking (and were later shown to be not dissimilar to the teaching of Advaita to which I eventually subscribed, although the latter are found in the Vedas, thousands of years prior to Kant). Firstly is his clear differentiation between what we can know – the world of appearances perceived through our senses, what he called the *phenomenal* realm – and what we can never know – how things 'really' are, what he called the *noumenal*.

He observed that our senses are limited. We can only see a narrow range of the electromagnetic spectrum for example and not radio waves or X-rays. We can only hear part of the range of sounds. We cannot smell with the sensitivity of a dog or navigate like birds or salmon. We have no senses at all that can detect magnetism or neutrinos for example. There are vast areas of the universe that we can only be aware of indirectly through instruments devised by science. If we do not have those instruments or science has not yet devised them, those areas of the universe simply do not exist for us. And even in those areas in which our senses do operate, what they tell us is translated by organs and brain into something totally alien to the "thing-in-itself" as he called the reality of an object. Sensory impressions can only be like other sensory impressions. They exist in the mind of the perceiver while the reality exists outside and is essentially independent of experience. The noumenal is thus 'transcendental' – hence the name given to his variety of metaphysics: 'Transcendental Idealism.' It is our minds that impose form upon the raw data of perception.

One consequence of this is that any explanation for the phenomenal world would have to lie outside of it and is therefore effectively unknowable. We can never know whether God exists; we are obliged to rely upon faith. In fact, Kant inferred that there must be a God in order to reward us in the next life for virtuous behavior in this one, since it was evident that immoral men often seemed to thrive in this life. If anyone expressed such a view now, we would think he was being ironic.

Furthermore, the concepts that we use to make sense of the world are just that – ideas in the mind – they have nothing to do with the way things really are. This applies even to those most fundamental concepts of all: space, time and causality (though he actually called these 'ways of looking at things' rather than concepts). He acknowledged that behavior in the phenomenal world follows the laws of science but did not accept that it therefore follows that we have no free will. He got around this by claiming that this operated in the noumenal realm.

In exercising our free will, he believed that we could and should use our reason in order to determine how to act. He thought that a valid reason would always be valid, and he proposed what he called the "Categorical Imperative", which says that we should act only according to maxims that we could wish to be universal laws – i.e. ask ourselves, "How would it be if everyone behaved like this?" 'Categorical' means that it should be done irrespective of any consideration of outcome, as opposed to a 'hypothetical' imperative, which would say that you must perform the action if you wish to achieve a particular outcome.

An example of this would be borrowing money from someone and making a false promise to pay it back. If we imagine what would happen if this were a general principle and everyone did it, it becomes obvious that no one would ever pay any attention to promises, particularly the person from whom we are trying to borrow. It would only work so long as we were making an exception, allowing ourselves to lie but no one else.

He believed that we only have to consider what our duty is in any given situation and need not consider what the possible outcomes might be or what we ourselves might want. If we have an obligation to do something then we should, as far as possible, try to comply with this. If not, then we can simply follow our natural inclination. Furthermore, when it comes to considerations of 'good and evil', he thought that the only thing that is good without qualification is good will.

Kant expressed his Categorical Imperative in another way: *"Act in such a way that you always treat humanity, whether in your own person or in the person of any other, never simply as a means but always at the same time as an end."* People are not things and a price cannot be placed upon the worth of a man. Acting towards someone (including oneself) in any way that is disrespectful, demeaning or even indifferent is effectively assuming that the recipient of the action has a low value and this makes such an action morally wrong.

Finally, in order to be considered 'moral' we must act because we know that it is the right thing to do (and his claim was that we simply know what is right in the same way that we know that bachelors are unmarried). If we perform an action because we want to or because we know we might be punished if we do not, then we are acting immorally. I.e. morality relates to the motive for action and not to the consequences.

Kant's differentiation between the world of appearances and the world of reality was built upon by a number of subsequent philosophers. It allows us to postulate our ideals as existing in this hidden world, where truth and God are found, and gives us a sense of purpose in striving to overcome the limitations of the perceived world. The alternative would be to admit that life is meaningless. Kant himself claimed that his philosophy *"criticized reason in order to make room for faith."* The fact that he had shown that it was impossible ever to know anything about an external world suggested a further step of denying its existence altogether. Everything might simply be a projection of our own mind, i.e. we don't simply formulate a meaning for external data but actually generate the data ourselves and impose the form at the same time. This would effectively be solipsism – the belief that only I exist – and Kant did not subscribe to this step.

Romanticism

Kant's noumenal consisted of the reality of mental *things* – plural – though we could never be objectively aware of them in any sense, and effectively acknowledged the existence of many minds as well as that of God himself. Kant was very influential, thought by many to have been the greatest of modern thinkers, and a number of philosophers attempted to build upon or revise his ideas, in particular to do away with his unknowable reality.

Johann Gottlieb Fichte was the first of these and he conceived of an absolute mind or ego, divided up into the relative egos of human personalities, which together were evolving. Objects or 'things in themselves' became redundant. History is explained, and our sense of meaning is gained, by reference to this absolute ego. Even supposedly straightforward explanatory accounts of his philosophy, however, are incomprehensible without attempting to read any of the original material (and possibly with, too, but I have no direct knowledge of this).

Friedrich Wilhelm Joseph von Schelling preferred not to eliminate the world completely, though he acknowledged that it could not be considered independent from the witnessing self. He thought that subject and object were one in a universal Nature and that reality is effectively the Absolute contemplating itself. "Nature reflects Consciousness," he said. Such ideas influenced contemporary poets such as Goethe in Germany and

Coleridge in England. Pantheism – God in everything – and Nature as a living unity appealed to their romantic sentiments. He is remembered particularly for asking the question as to why there is something rather than nothing.

Hegel

In the continuing attempt to simplify the view of things, his more prominent contemporary Hegel thought that reality must consist of only one thing, a single mind or 'Absolute.' Beginningless and endless, this contains all of the infinite possibilities but is continually changing and realizing its potentialities. We ourselves are a part or form of this as are the rest of the apparently separate things in the universe.

History, said Hegel, is effectively a record of this process of the universal mind or spirit moving towards ultimate perfection. What happens is that any given state of society is less than perfect, containing within itself certain contradictions. Some changes are needed in order to resolve these and this brings about a new state that provides solutions for the faults of the former. Now there are problems by having moved too far in the other direction and there is a need to resolve the situation by combining the positive aspects of the former two states. The overall process was called 'dialectic' after the technique of question and answer used by Socrates to elicit the truth. Hegel used this procedure to arrive at his belief in the Absolute.

The classical view of what is meant by 'freedom' for an individual is the ability to make choices in one's own life without being influenced by society. Hegel thought this naïve, recognizing that people's attitudes are constantly being influenced by others so that, often, what we choose is what the influential people of the time want us to choose, which is no freedom at all. Of course they didn't have TV and Google's 'push' technology telling us that we could not be happy unless we smoked Hamlet cigars in those days but Hegel was fully aware of the principle. He believed that this effect had been in existence throughout history and that the only way out was for us to take control of these forces ourselves.

We should stop thinking of others as competitors and potential enemies, and recognize that we are all reasoning beings with essentially similar aims. Unlike Kant, however, he did not think that there needed to be a conflict between what we ought to do and what we want to do. He believed that a society based on reason could function such that each person could seek his or her own fulfillment while still dutifully acting for the good of all. We could reach a compromise between what we want for ourselves as part of our society at this particular time and what reason tells us is our duty. There need be no conflict, as Kant had said would always be the case. Though this all sounds very well, his philosophy was taken up by Marx and led directly to Lenin and Communism, though all of this came about by a willful misinterpreting of what Hegel had said (perhaps not so surprising, since his books are reported to be notoriously difficult to understand!).

Schopenhauer

Arthur Schopenhauer was perhaps the most well-known thinker to continue the line of thought initiated by Kant. His first enhancement was to suggest that the 'noumenal' realm of 'things in themselves' could not in fact consist of *plural* things. One 'thing' must be separate from another 'thing', either in time or in space, in order for us to be aware of two 'things.' If there were not this separation, we would only be aware of *one* thing. Accordingly, since time and space do not exist in reality, number cannot have any relevance. In fact, since causality is also just our way of explaining happenings in the world of appearances, the noumenal could not in any sense *cause* the phenomenal.

In fact, the phenomenal world must just be another way of looking at the noumenal. Everything that we see is just a manifestation of this undifferentiated reality, including ourselves of course. There can be no such thing therefore as meaning or purpose, whether of our own lives or of the universe. In a sense, it is all an illusion. There is much in common with a number of Eastern religions here, including some branches of Buddhism, Hinduism, Taoism, Sufism etc. and Schopenhauer did in fact have some exposure to these, though supposedly after he had developed his own ideas.

His outlook was notoriously pessimistic and he appeared to be obsessed with the miseries of life and the unpleasantness of its inhabitants, with each striving to survive at the expense of everyone else. Our moral aim, he said, should be to minimize the suffering of others by feeling compassion for them. This could not be an imperative, as Kant had suggested, since we had to act from our own nature; moral goodness cannot be taught or commanded.

There has to be a reason for everything that exists or happens, he said in his earliest work, contradicting people such as Hume, who said that some things simply *are* and we can never say why. In the case of happenings in the world, these have physical explanations; logical explanations exist for truths prior to our experience or mathematical ones for such things as geometrical demonstrations. Our own actions have moral reasons. Although we cannot perceive the noumenal in the usual sense, he claimed that we were effectively aware of it through our 'Will to live', which is the noumenal aspect of our activities in the phenomenal world. The universe itself in its merely apparent diversity is in fact the outward manifestation of the cosmic 'Will to exist.'

The only reasonable place to go to simplify things even further is solipsism. I could try to go further and claim that even I do not exist but then who would be making the denial? But while this has been discussed by philosophers, none seems to have seriously maintained it as an outlook.

Marx

As noted earlier, Hegel's philosophy was very influential with Marx, whose ideas are the basis of the intellectual foundation of Communism. In particular, he accepted Hegel's concept of reality as an ongoing dialectic process, which could be monitored through a study of history, and which would continue to evolve until there were no further internal contradictions needing resolution. Not until this was achieved would true freedom and fulfillment be possible for man. He believed that the sort of society that would bring this about would be one in which individuals acted together rather than independently. Marx did not, however, agree with Hegel's concept of a spiritual 'Absolute.' Any form of religious belief or pursuit was seen as an attempt to escape from the meaninglessness that life had become.

He believed that matter, in the sense of man's relation to it, was the driving force behind progress, and this meant that subjects such as the production and distribution of goods, and the economics of this, became extremely important. Thus he would have argued that socialism was simply the point that had been reached in the process of evolution, not something that he was specifically advocating, though his personal commitment to the 'revolution' is apparent in his writing. But all of this is a matter of politics and was advocated at the expense of ethical considerations.

So-called progress had produced a world of technology but man was being controlled by this instead of controlling it (and this is over 150 years ago!). He was being alienated from the true values of life, such as friendship and culture, and instead was being conned into desiring the products themselves. In this process, he felt that he himself was becoming dehumanized. Most of us probably now appreciate that cars, DVDs and mobile phones are mere 'things' that can never bring happiness or fulfillment. And yet much of today's generation seems to be trapped in a downward spiral of dependence upon the next fix from the purveyors of our material society.

Communism was inevitable as far as he was concerned and what any individual might want was not a consideration. It would represent the final synthesis of the then-current conflict between the working class, who actually produced the goods, and the capitalist employers who owned the means of production, and everyone would then be happy. The means of production would be jointly owned and be used in everyone's interest. For him, then, the purpose was clear and achievable – the bringing about of a better world. Unfortunately, as we all now know, these good ideas were unrealizable in practice and led only to far worse repression and lack of individual freedom. It just took a long time and considerable suffering before this was finally accepted by most people.

Nietzsche

Friedrich Nietzsche began his philosophical career as a disciple of Schopenhauer but did not share the latter's pessimism and eventually diverged drastically when he decided that the world was the only reality. He claimed that there was no point at all in searching for some idealized spiritual truth since none existed. We should aim to realize our potential within this life since that is all there is. He saw that society was descending into nihilism and that the existing philosophies and religions were powerless to prevent it. A new ethos was needed. He was highly suspicious of absolutes with respect to truth or knowledge, suggesting that there are no real facts, only interpretations and his books tend to make suggestions (often in metaphorical form) rather than lay down rigorous principles.

He believed that the moral values that had been passed down to us from earlier generations were necessarily outdated. Man was continually evolving, with the stronger overcoming the weaker, and it was necessary that our standards should evolve with us. Why pay any attention to outmoded religious principles and rules of conduct when we no longer believe in them? – God is dead. Since the strong overcome the weak as a natural part of progress, the strong should determine their own values and not be held back by any notion of equality with the mediocre masses. Meaning must be generated from within, not from some presumed external deity. Men are certainly not 'equal.' We should be free to realize our full potential and become 'supermen.' He valued passion, anger and adventure, advocated discipline and strength of will, and regarded the compassion of Christianity with contempt. *"Christianity,"* he said, *"breaks the spirit of the strong and poisons their noble instincts so that they perish through self-loathing."*

He despised the Christian ideals of goodness, such as loving one's fellow man, claiming that this was simply the outcome of fear and said that we should openly display the scorn that we really feel. His idealized man was a ruthless hero, seeking only more power, treating others as inferior, especially women, who should be treated as property and were only *"for the recreation of the warrior"*; we should *"go to them with a whip."*

His ideas affected politics, in particular the Nationalism of Hitler, though Nietzsche himself did not support the principles of Nazism. He also saw art as being of great importance in transforming ourselves and the world. This inevitably influenced literature (e.g. Strindberg, Shaw, Mann, Hesse and Camus), music (e.g. Mahler and Richard Strauss – who named one of his most famous tone-poems after Nietzsche's literary-philosophical work *Also sprach Zarathustra*) and other philosophers (e.g. Sartre). But the idea that only the happiness of a few really matters – those who happen to be strong in body and will or who happen to be born into rich and influential families – that these few are in some way superior, scarcely seems reasonable to the modern mind. This was the sort of society that existed in Egypt at the time of the Pharaohs, with an elite few living in luxury and the majority enslaved to support them. There are, no doubt, still some today who would want such a world... but only as long as they are amongst the rulers.

But Nietzsche was wide of the mark when he set his aims. His ideals were mistaken, participating in those aspects of man's nature that are part of his limitations. He was seeking the empowerment of the ego, not the realization of his true nature. His is the way of fear and led the man himself to insanity at the age of 44.

Bentham and Utilitarianism

When deciding whether an action should be deemed good or bad (as opposed to whether it is something we ourselves *want* to do), people will sometimes try to calculate whether the result will benefit the majority. This principle was expressed in the 18th century by Francis Hutcheson: "*That action is best which procures the greatest happiness for the greatest numbers.*" It is effectively the opposite of what Kant was saying. Whereas he insisted that it was the motive alone that determined whether an act should be deemed to be 'good' and that we should act from a sense of duty, Hutcheson was claiming that motives were ultimately irrelevant, it was the outcome alone that mattered.

Two philosophers in particular were responsible for developing and propagating these ideas and thereby influencing many people's attitude towards morality. The first was Jeremy Bentham, who is generally regarded as the originator of so-called 'Utilitarianism', which says that conduct is right or wrong according to its tendency to produce favorable or unfavorable consequences for the people who are affected by it. It was given this name because actions are judged on the basis of their 'utility' or usefulness in bringing about good or benefit of some kind, as opposed to evil or unhappiness.

Bentham was effectively a social reformer rather than a philosopher and his interest lay in areas such as 'making the punishment fit the crime' and changing the educational system.

His view of punishment is that it prevents *future* crime (thus minimizing future misery for everyone) rather than providing a penalty for past action. It might be in the best interest of everyone else if I do not steal from them but it only becomes in my best interest as well if there is a law imposing punishment if I steal. He was also in favor of less severe penalties – juries would often refuse to convict a criminal of a relatively minor crime if there was the threat of his being sentenced to death.

As perceived by Bentham, the results that were important were pleasure and pain. These were terms that everyone understood. The best actions of all are those that bring happiness to the greatest number of people. Previously existing religious traditions or social conventions should obviously be ignored in this context. Even if they may once have satisfied the majority, they mostly no longer do so – obviously Puritanism or the self-righteous and often hypocritical values of Victorian society will no longer appeal to twenty-first century mores. The individual is no longer able to look to parents, church or tradition as sources for constructing meaning in his life (unless such values are imposed by a repressive regime).

Though the principles will be more obvious than say Kant's deontological (i.e. duty-based) ones, they will nevertheless not necessarily appeal to most people. Why should I vote for what the majority want to do if I want to do something different? If pleasure is the most important goal in life, why should I choose something that will bring me pain?

John Stuart Mill

John Stuart Mill continued the Utilitarian trend but he did not agree with Bentham's attempts to quantify the happiness of the greatest number. It is not enough to define degrees of pleasure or relative probabilities of their occurrence. Some pleasures, he said, were more 'worthy' than others. *"It is better to be a man dissatisfied than a pig satisfied,"* he claimed. But it is not possible to quantify such things; rather they are 'qualities' that raise man above the level of animals.

He believed that individuals should be allowed to do as they liked providing that they did not cause harm to others. He did not accept that we were free to *choose* any course of action. We are limited in what we can do by our own natures and by external circumstance. As to what we *ought* to do, the doctrine of Utilitarianism is effectively a return to that of the Epicureans in Ancient Greece. Pleasure is what matters (i.e. the philosophy of 'hedonism') and the important thing is the *result* of what we do, not the *motive* for doing it (this is called the 'Consequentialist' theory). If we have a 'good' motive, we will be morally praiseworthy but whether the act itself is morally good or bad is purely dependent upon the outcome. The results, of course, could be good for me and/or good for others. The best of all would be if it could be beneficial for everyone but, since this is rarely the case, I am likely to have motives for one rather than the other. If I want the best for myself, this is *egoistic*, if for others it is *altruistic*. Mill thought that everyone should be treated alike, including ourselves. This is called *universalistic*.

Utilitarianism is in conflict with more traditional views of morality when it is only interested in pleasure as an outcome, whether for me or others. It would always be the case, for example, that one should tell a lie if convinced that this would bring happiness (or minimize pain) for the majority. Consequently, if everyone behaved in this way we would never know whether someone was telling the truth. Later philosophers suggested that the precepts should be modified. It was suggested that, in the case of two alternative courses of action, if both are thought likely to produce equivalent levels of pleasure, we should choose that action which is traditionally moral, for example more open and honest, more in keeping with the dignity of man and so on. But this is really recognition of the inability of Utilitarianism to cope with such issues and an implicit admission of its failure as a guide to action.

Once you begin to think deeply about the practical details of behaving in this way, the values of laws and moral principles become apparent and it is seen to be difficult or impossible to act without deceiving others or even oneself – and this is one of the characteristics of what we normally call 'immorality.'

Before leaving JS Mill, it is worth mentioning his conclusions regarding happiness. He acknowledged that this was the principal aim of our lives but claimed that it should never be sought as such. He thought that it only ever came about as a sort of side effect while we were actually doing something else or seeking some entirely separate result. All of which makes the philosophy of hedonism somewhat incongruous as well as the idea of Consequentialism!

William James and Pragmatism

Developed originally in America, and to some extent in rebellion against the metaphysical theories current in Europe at the time (especially Idealism), Pragmatism is effectively a method for determining the worth of philosophical problems and their proposed solutions. What was thought to matter was not all of the intellectual speculation and theorizing usually associated with philosophy but the practical worth at the end of the day. Is a theory actually of any use to us in our day-to-day life? Will it make any difference to me if I follow it or am even aware of its existence? The word 'pragmatic' has now passed into everyday usage as referring to an approach that actually works.

The original ideas were developed by CS Peirce, who saw himself as following up the system devised by Kant. He thought the only purpose of philosophy to begin with was to solve problems that we actually encounter. We should then use the scientific method to enquire into the problem, drawing up hypotheses, experiments to test them and so on. Once we have an answer that gets us over the original problem we should simply stop there. A proposition is 'true' if everyone who investigates sufficiently thoroughly comes to the same conclusion.

His ideas were promoted and enhanced by William James, the psychologist and brother of Henry, the novelist. James thought that a philosophical doctrine was worthwhile, and in a sense 'true', if its practice led to people's happiness. He did not accept that an idea could somehow be true without taking into account our experience. Here, he disagreed with Plato, who had said that ideas were absolutely true or false, irrespective of whether anyone knew it. According to the Pragmatists, it is true if it works. It is neither true nor false to begin with but acquires one of those properties when we actually try it in practice.

This is not quite as ridiculous as it may at first sound. Newton's laws of motion for example were initially regarded as universally true because they worked. After Einstein, however, and the Michelson-Morley experiments to investigate the speed of light, it was discovered that they did not give the correct results whereas the new Theory of Special Relativity did. Accordingly, in such situations, Newton's laws became false since they did not work and Einstein's became true.

Furthermore, metaphysical beliefs which afford no clear benefit whether we believe in them or not are not worthy of our attention (says the Pragmatist). According to this, it might be argued that it makes no sense for us to investigate the various theories that attempt to explain the nature of reality. The problems that face us in our everyday lives remain the same regardless. Obviously, I cannot subscribe to this conclusion!

Similarly, argued James, any idea is true if it helps us to live our lives. If belief in God makes life easier to accept, leads to people behaving better towards each other and so on, then *it* is true. This supporting argument for God was condemned by the Pope. As Bertrand Russell pointed out, the same argument would show that Santa Claus also exists. Belief in God is *not* the same as existence of God.

Clearly, Pragmatism does not offer a consistent and satisfactory basis for behavior from a moral point of view either. If I am seriously financially challenged and obliged to repay some debts, then meeting you in a dark alley and liberating you from your wallet may well 'work' for me but it is doubtful that anyone, especially you, would think it 'right' or 'good' in any sense.

William James was also responsible for another, unrelated theory concerning the existence (or not) of consciousness. The traditional view of experience was that there is a 'knower', a process of 'knowing' and an object (be it gross or subtle) that is 'known.' James denied that this subject-object dualism was fundamental. He did not accept the existence of a thing called Consciousness and thought instead that everything is 'made out of' experience. Out of this mass of experience, we differentiate the various aspects such as ourselves, food and partners. Nothing is fixed; we simply do whatever is appropriate to make sense of the world as it appears at any given instant and the experience develops accordingly, giving rise to a new differentiation.

Logic and Language

Philosophy lost its sense of direction in many ways in the twentieth century, with some of the best minds in the world devoting themselves to analyzing sentence structure and meaning. It began with the German Gottlob Frege stating that our investigations ought to be based upon logic rather than epistemology. His investigations related mostly to mathematics, trying to demonstrate its axioms logically. Bertrand Russell had been working on similar problems independently and he took over the ideas, attempting to apply them more widely. He wanted to prove that all of our knowledge comes from experience. What he found was that, once he began to analyze the construction of some of our statements, he was able to uncover logical errors. When these were removed and the statements made correctly, the problems that were thought to have been implicit were removed.

Wittgenstein

Ludwig Wittgenstein believed that philosophers had to confine their investigations to the phenomenal world, having accepted the pronouncement of Kant that reality was forever beyond our objective understanding. In the book that he eventually managed to get published, which goes by the wonderful name of *Tractatus Logico-Philosophicus*, he attempted to define the relationship between language and the world that it purported to describe, highlighting its function, mechanism and limitations. He believed at the time that in doing this he had clarified the nature of philosophy completely so that no further work would ever be needed.

In his later life he virtually rejected all of this work and began again, though nothing more was published until after his death. Wittgenstein's family, incidentally, was one of the richest in Europe at the time and he could have inherited all of this and lived a life of luxury. Instead he refused any of it and spent much of his life working hard for a relatively low income in various jobs until he was eventually recognized as a truly great philosopher and offered a post at Cambridge University.

The *Tractatus* states that we can only speak meaningfully about something if there is a direct correspondence between our words and statements, and the actual objects and relationships in the world. Attempts to talk about God, emotional problems and so on, where there are no concrete things to which the language can relate, are ultimately meaningless. He ends the work with the oft-quoted statement: *"Whereof we cannot speak, thereof we should remain silent."*

These beginnings led on to a movement called 'Logical Positivism' which claimed that only those statements that could be verified were actually meaningful and its adherents attempted to use scientific standards to elucidate meaning. One of the main proponents, AJ Ayer, believed that the statements that we make must be verifiable either by reference to experience or by virtue of the meanings of the constituent words and the grammar of the sentence. If a statement cannot be verified in either of these two ways then it must be meaningless. Much of what earlier philosophers had written on the subject of religion and ethics, for example, fell into this third category, it was claimed! To say that something is good means nothing more than that I approve of it. One of the members of the so-called Vienna Circle that originated Logical Positivism, Herbert Feigl, said that, *"Philosophy is the disease of which it should be the cure."*

These tenets were later realized to have been unreasonable and the movement was displaced by 'Linguistic Analysis', which used a more common-sense approach. The idea here was that each discipline and specialization has its own vocabulary and "language games", as Wittgenstein later described them, so that it was necessary to restrict usage of a particular mode to the area in which it was applicable. Problems arise when we fail to do this and use an inappropriate way to express ourselves. The function of the philosopher is to disentangle the misuse of language and express the situation in a common-sense manner, the result being that there is now no longer a problem. At least that was the theory!

Wittgenstein now realized that the meaning of words was not fixed such that they were always used to convey a single reality. Instead, their meaning varies according to the context in which they are used together with the nature of the speaker and listener. In order to understand what is being said, all of these have to be taken into consideration. Furthermore, languages develop and exist purely for communication. We have to use words according to the rules that have been agreed within the frame of reference in which the communication is taking place and language can only have meaning in such a context, i.e. we could not have a 'private language' used only by ourselves for thinking.

Phenomenology

This movement began in the late nineteenth century as a theory of knowledge that attempted to reinstate science and bring in the modern findings from psychology and sociology to supplant the subjectivity that had predominated until then with the German Idealists. In particular, they wished to understand the nature of awareness, differentiating between mental and non-mental realms. Edmund Husserl, who was the teacher of Martin Heidegger (below), is generally credited with establishing the movement. It was acknowledged that we could not know that objects exist independent of our awareness of them but also that it cannot be denied that we are conscious of 'things.' Phenomenology endeavored to start from this point and attempt to analyze our experience without making any further assumptions. It subsequently merged into Existentialism.

Maurice Merleau-Ponty was particularly interested in perception and the nature of the perceiving entity and 'object' of perception. He disliked both the empiricist and idealist approaches and spent much of his time attacking all dualist concepts such as the mind-matter division of Descartes. There cannot be any totally objective perception of the world, he said, because our perceptual apparatus is itself part of the world. Whenever we see something, what we 'see' comes along with everything else that we already know and the perception itself is the sum total of all of this. We can never see a chair, for example, without the awareness of its purpose as something for sitting on. The origin of our belief in a separate world derives from our thinking of 'ourselves' as other than the body that we apparently inhabit. We *are* our bodies, he said, and the mind cannot be separated from them.

Merleau-Ponty, like Wittgenstein before him, had second

thoughts in his later life and attempted to rewrite his philosophy. In particular, he felt that his earlier work still suffered from the dualistic point of view of the philosopher attempting to describe a philosophy of consciousness. He really wanted to understand the nature of 'being' (the study that is called 'ontology' in philosophy). His previous ideas had incorporated the idea of a consciousness that exists prior to thought or language and he now wanted to deny this. Language thus came to play a much more important role.

Existentialism

The term derives from the Danish (and German) *Existenz* that was used by the philosopher Søren Kierkegaard to refer to the essential, subjective nature of our existence – our experience as an individual. (The movement did not come to be recognized as such until much later with the Frenchman Jean-Paul Sartre.) Kierkegaard felt that our emotions were just as important as our capacity for reason. In his own life, he frequently suffered from severe depression, a malady that we perhaps naively tend to associate with the often pessimistic views expressed in the novels of Sartre and Camus. In his philosophy too, Kierkegaard wrote of how freedom ultimately leads to despair. He criticized Hegel's philosophy for not taking account of the fundamental fact of human life, namely our experience as individuals. He still considered that it was our relationship with God that mattered most, though he was very critical of organized religion. We should turn our thoughts inward and appreciate our insignificance in His sight.

To the extent that we allow our choices in life to be dictated by preferences, experience, advice from others or other criteria, our future is predetermined. But we cannot escape choice and so should endeavor to make this from a basis of doubt, making a 'leap of faith' and accepting responsibility for our action. It cannot be meaningful simply to rely upon whatever situations, objects and people just happen to come our way. The model for such a life is that of Christ. Only by living in such a way can man achieve true satisfaction and feel that his existence is meaningful. The pursuit of pleasure or blindly following what is perceived to be one's duty both eventually pall and lead to despair. *"The thing is,"* he said, *"to find a truth which is true for me, to find the idea for which I can live and die."* There is no doubt that Kierkegaard at least very much wanted to find a meaning to his life!

Heidegger

Martin Heidegger is generally regarded as the founder of Existentialism, though he himself claimed not to be an Existentialist, saying that it was 'being' rather than the person that was important. He followed Kierkegaard in believing that the fundamental fact of our lives is our individuality and essential isolation. Kierkegaard had called it 'angst', the basic dread or anxiety we feel in the face of inherent uncertainty and the lack of control that we experience regarding ourselves and our future. Heidegger used the same term to describe our anxiety relating to the responsibility that we have to take for 'being here' in this life. Our essential entity he called "dasein" (to be there), meaning that we are not isolated from the world, observing it dispassionately, but intimately involved and forever interacting with it in one way or another. Thus it is incorrect to attempt to describe an external world of objects separate from ourselves. There are really just 'beings-in-the-world.'

We find ourselves here, he said, in a particular country, with a family background that was not of our choosing, and that is where we start from. We can either accept all of this, believing ourselves to be no different from everyone else and simply living from day to day or, motivated by our angst, we can strive to realize our potential as individuals. This latter mode is the only authentic way of life. We may not succeed but this is the only environment available to us so that our meaning and purpose have to be found within this context.

His view was that it would be meaningless to say that we wanted to be in the situation of a millionaire and, since we are not, therefore we are not free. Even the beggar in the street is free if he accepts what he is and tries to change it. There are always choices, and freedom lies in accepting one's limitations and making a choice out of those that are available. There cannot be a formula for providing us with purpose and meaning. It is for each individual, in his own particular situation, to make a choice and commit to it and this alone will provide meaning for that individual. This situation is ongoing for the whole of our lives. If an actual answer were compelled for the question as to what makes life worth living, the answer would have to be – nothing.

Before our birth, he claimed, we were nothing and after our death we will be nothing. Death brings an end to all possibilities and, in a sense, makes everything meaningless. We have to face this fact, accept responsibility for our life here and now, and then act without procrastination. Our lives are in a sense defined by the 'nothingness' that forever threatens in the background.

Sartre

Jean-Paul Sartre was most concerned with the freedom of the individual. We determine and define our own lives through the choices that we make. We can either ignore this responsibility, telling ourselves that we are forced to act as we do by our circumstances, society etc. or we can make a 'commitment' and live life to the full. The choices that I make 'for myself' are also in part determining the development of humanity as a whole, since these choices will always either agree or disagree with the choices of others and bring about harmony or discord. The meaning of our lives and 'our' world are effectively created through our moment to moment choices. That entails responsibility, and realization of this brings the 'angst' to which Kierkegaard had referred. There is no one who can tell us what to do and, inevitably, we must encounter failure from time to time. This can lead to despair. It is this danger that has led to people often associating Existentialism with depression and the darker emotions of life.

Sartre also said that we need the feedback from others in order to understand ourselves. In moments of embarrassment, for example, it is the fact that our behavior is noticed by others that makes us aware of ourselves objectively. And in such a situation, we are caused to label ourselves in some way and these activities are instrumental in defining ourselves as a separate ego.

Albert Camus, the Nobel Prize-winning novelist, was also an Existentialist. (Sartre was nominated for the Nobel Prize, too, but declined to accept.) He believed that there is no meaning at all in the universe and our attempts to make any sense of our lives is consequently 'absurd.' In one of his philosophical essays, he compares our situation to that of the character Sisyphus from Greek mythology, whose sentence in hell was repeatedly to push a boulder up to the top of a mountain, from which it always rolled down again. His recourse to cope with the punishment is scorn:

Sisyphus, proletarian of the gods, powerless and rebellious, knows the whole extent of his wretched condition; it is what he thinks of during his descent. The lucidity that was to constitute his torture at the same time crowns his victory. There is no fate that cannot be surmounted by scorn.

Some Key Issues

Having looked briefly at the history of Western philosophy and highlighted the major figures and the thinking that seemed to me most relevant in a search for meaning, I would now like to look in a bit more detail at several specific areas of study that seem especially significant.

Morality

How we 'ought' to behave depends upon what we and others believe. We accept that some things are good and others bad but we may have difficulty deciding whether such beliefs are somehow absolute or whether they are simply a set of related ideas inculcated by our family, peers and society at large. Cynically, it often seems to be the case that what is deemed to be *right* depends upon who is speaking. And if we believe that we are each independent individuals with our own particular needs and ambitions, this is inevitable. The word 'good' simply means that I like it (a good wine) or I approve of it (a good lawyer). In this second case, we might also be using the word in the sense of someone who is proficient in their work, in which case we might have to concede that someone is a good burglar. None of these senses seems appropriate when thinking about how we should behave.

Statements about how we *ought* to act do not seem to express any factual information and, if you think about them, it is not really clear what exactly they are saying. If you say that it is dangerous to drink and drive, I can understand that you are suggesting that I might have an accident and injure myself or someone else. But if you say that it is *wrong*, what exactly is it that you are claiming and can you additionally say that the statement is *true*? The 'Emotive' theory of ethics claims that such statements merely express the feelings of the person making them. Similarly, to say that something is 'good' is a personal opinion and is not saying anything in any way objectively verifiable. It is even quite possible that what you consider to be good (going to a party, for example), I would think to be absolutely awful![†]

Another way in which the terms 'good' and 'bad' are used is in respect of how well they perform the function for which we intend to use them. Thus one person might think a 'good' car is one that has a convertible roof and goes from 0–60mph in 5 seconds whereas another might insist that it does 50mpg and will hold a family of six and all their luggage. A 'good' dog might be one that is faithful and a deterrent to burglars or one that is succulent and feeds the whole family, depending upon which country you live in. If we are unsure of the intended function, the use of these terms might not seem appropriate. If someone points to a stone and says that it is a 'good' stone, we might wonder what on earth they are talking about until we realize that they are looking for something to skim across the surface of a lake. But this is obviously not the context in which Plato was using the word in his quest for the Form of the Good. If we are suggesting that we, as human beings, ought to be good, we are unlikely to have any specific function in mind.

Nor does it seem reasonable to accept some sort of majority opinion, though the Sophists, for example, believed that morality was relative to the society and time and not an absolute thing at all. People can be ill-informed about a subject, and also attitudes change over time. At the time of the Sophists, slavery was perfectly acceptable and would not even have been considered to be a moral issue. But it does seem that there should be some sort of objectivity involved. It does not seem right that a thing be deemed good simply because you approve of it or consider it to be desirable. In fact, the British philosopher GE Moore at the beginning of the twentieth century claimed that it was not possible to define terms such as 'good' at all. We can talk about how it is related to other concepts but not pin it down in any absolute sense.

Many theories have been constructed over the past two and a half thousand years (of recorded Western philosophy) to attempt to make sense of all of this and provide us with a reasoned description of how we ought to behave. Unfortunately there is no book of certain rules on the subject and people will disagree about who should be regarded as an expert on the matter. The following is just a sprinkling of some of those ideas. If you want to investigate the subject in detail, prepare yourself for an awful lot of reading!

The attempts to formulate some sort of philosophy relating to how we 'ought' to act may in fact have begun, in the West at least, with the Sophists in Greece around the fifth century BC. These philosophers did not hold any specific set of beliefs but were very well informed on a wide range of subjects and able to talk knowledgeably about them. The term has come to be used to refer to someone who is able to use arguments cleverly and often fallaciously to convince others of a particular point of view. Thus it was thought at the time that such people would be able to make a case for either of two opposite courses of action being the right thing to do, making it impossible to agree to any single set of moral standards. The idea that this might actually be true must have stimulated later philosophers to set about trying to analyze the situation and try to formulate some acceptable guidelines. And such attempts have continued ever since!

Some people think that, in some way, there effectively *are* rules that define how we ought to behave and that we can discover what these rules are. This study is called *Normative Ethics*, and once the rules have been established we can use *Applied Ethics* to relate them to our various fields of action such as doctors with their patients or politicians in a government and so on. If we don't believe that there can be any laws as such, so that we are not actually under obligation to act in any one way rather than another, we can still attempt to set standards and ask questions about the applicability of these to various activities. This would be the study of *Meta-ethics*.

One possibility might be that morality exists as absolute truths – so-called *Moral Realism* or *Ethical Absolutism*. Just as we believe that 1+1=2 must always be true, so perhaps it is somehow necessarily true that we should not kill another human being. This is effectively what Plato believed, with the truths somehow existing in the world of Forms. We discover these principles through philosophical insights rather than inventing them or devising them to suit our own purpose. And they necessarily apply to everyone irrespective of their inclinations or the nature of the society in which they live. In the absence of absolute certainty regarding these truths, we are obliged to act according to what we think they are.

In this view of morality, things are 'good' irrespective of whether a God decrees them. We ought to be able to see that 'loving our neighbor', for example, is going to be beneficial to ourselves and society, whereas committing adultery is likely to upset a few people. We should not really need any outside agency to endorse such attitudes.

Alternatively, the ways in which we should act might have been ordained by God, as in the tablets of the Ten Commandments found by Moses. (Some wit recently referred to these as the Ten Suggestions, in recognition of their lack of regard by modern society – few people these days can actually list more than two or three of them.) We might call this *Divine Command*. This implies that we are unable fully to understand moral principles unless we believe in God. In fact, people who take this stance argue that morality makes no sense unless there is a God to lay down the standards. It also implies that God could command something that now seems abhorrent to us and we would have to accept it as a new standard of behavior. Some gods in the past have demanded human sacrifices, for example. Or at least so their priests have told us!

But maybe this possibility is effectively the same as the first option since we cannot validate it in any scientifically acceptable manner. In either case, the implication is that there exists a universally applicable, absolute set of rules to direct our behavior, even though these might change at any moment at the whim of a God. There is also the very significant problem as to how we are to ascertain what God's will happens to be at any given moment. If we hear him telling us, how do we know we are not delusional schizophrenics? If we want to read what His instructions are, to which book should we refer? In any case, if we follow such rules because we want to go to heaven or are afraid that God will punish us if we don't, this is no longer morality but self-interest.

The optimum ways of behaving may simply have been worked out through practice and discussion in order for people to coexist in society – so-called *Moral Relativism*. According to this approach, the attitudes that have been found to work best are the ones that parents pass on to their children and they become traditional. This suggests that behavior should be adapted so as to suit the particular community, or even individual, at that particular time – i.e. any rules are only relative.

If you believe that right and wrong are something that you either know or decide for yourself according to your conscience, irrespective of what the laws happen to be or what others might think, this is *Individual Relativism*. If we relate everything to our particular society or religion, it is called *Social Relativism* and the individual's point of view is then merely an opinion. For either of these stances it is not possible to say anything more than that the individual or group thinks that X is right or Y is wrong. If another individual or group says the opposite, then that is simply how it *is* for them. There is no way of arbitrating between them. For anyone who has views such as that Hitler's killing of the Jews was wrong *absolutely*, moral relativism is not acceptable.

Perhaps there are no real rules at all and we should use our own intuition and self-interest to make a decision. What is 'good' is simply what I want. What would be the point of pursuing particular ends unless I thought this? This is the position of *Moral Skepticism* or *Ethical Nihilism*. If we find it difficult to accept the notion of a realm in which ideal Forms exist and do not believe in a God who could give us commandments, then clearly moral principles cannot be objective in any sense. Some people help others while some steal from them; it's just their nature and who are we to say that one way is 'right' and another 'wrong'? But strictly speaking, doing something because we want to or because the outcome benefits us, irrespective of what anyone else wants or how it affects them, is not really a moral position at all, as the word is usually understood.

The ins and outs of these four main ways of viewing morality can be argued endlessly. For example, since there can never be any objective validation, we have to ask how we can ever know that we have discovered a moral truth. People once used to believe that slavery was perfectly OK and might well have argued that it was an absolute truth rather than simply a belief relative to that particular time and society. When children grow up having particular ways of looking at things impressed upon them, these become fundamental to their outlook on life. How are we to differentiate these two examples? Is it not always possible that someone could come along with more persuasive arguments and change one's own opinions? Indeed, we know (probably from our own experience) that this does indeed happen. Look how the 'boy next door' became a suicide bomber!

Some philosophers have suggested that the only sensible ethic is one that says we should do whatever it is that has the greatest possibility of benefiting us personally. This theory recognizes the fact that most people tend to be selfishly motivated. If we have evolved according to Darwinian principles then whatever helps us (i.e. our genes) to survive and propagate is effectively *good*; it does not really make any sense to attempt to define the word in any other way.

This would, however, mean that it ought to be acceptable and in no way morally reprehensible to rob or even kill others if we clearly benefited thereby (and did not get caught). This is the position known as *Ethical Egoism* and one presumes that people such as Saddam Hussein subscribed to it. In the long run it does not seem to work, not least because it upsets a lot of other people! It also has somewhat discomfiting side effects such as not knowing who your friends are. One can imagine that a long-term policy along these lines might bring lots of material possessions but it would be unlikely to bring any happiness.

At the opposite extreme is the theory that what is *right* is whatever action benefits everyone else, irrespective of how it might affect us. This is called *Ethical Altruism* and it probably does not appeal to very many, since most will feel that they ought to get something out of their own actions too – otherwise what would be the point? Pragmatically, a world of ethical altruists could never exist – the species would have died out long ago. In between the two is the Utilitarian viewpoint that was mentioned earlier. But this would still condemn totally selfish and passive activities, such as watching TV, since we could be spending our time benefiting ourselves and others in a positive way.

There are still many people who would claim that *good* actions are those that are in accordance with the will of God. But what exactly does this mean? It might mean that God would prefer it if people behaved in a certain way or it could mean that believers are motivated to act in a certain way, whereas nonbelievers would only do so by accident. Finally, it could mean that specific modes of behavior have somehow been declared as good and if we do not follow these rules we had better watch out.

It is very difficult to argue with such people and I would recommend from experience that you do not try. It is not, please note, that I do not respect their views; it is simply that there can be no agreed point of departure on which to base the discussion. The 'Will of God' is simply not amenable to verification unless you, too, accept the stated authority, be it the Bible or other scripture, a priest or other holy man or your own conscience. As with all such unprovable ideas, philosophers have amused themselves thinking of arguments for and against, and anyone interested can pursue them.

In any case, without being too cynical about this, it does seem to be the case that religions used often simply to take the moral guidelines that had been worked out by society and claim them as their own, effectively giving them divine approval. In the days when the church had supreme authority, this would have been a natural thing to do, reinforcing both society and themselves as moral arbiters.

Our society has evolved from ones that were considerably influenced by theological ideals. In mediaeval times, if you did not behave according to the laws supposedly decreed by God, you had better watch out. People were obliged to appear publicly to believe things that they knew were not actually true. One of the most famous examples was that of Galileo, who had to recant his discovery that the earth went around the sun, and not vice versa as Ptolemy had proposed and as was still upheld by the church.

Nowadays, there are still large numbers of people who, even if they do not entirely accept all of the claims made by their religion and no longer recognize it as an authority for their everyday behavior, nevertheless pay lip service. And sentiments such as 'love thy neighbor as thyself' do seem to contain great wisdom, finding a balance between the two extremes given above.

But with all of our values no longer 'supplied' by religion, people have been forced to develop them for themselves. In the absence of expert guidance, the principal influence now tends to be the media and we have such ridiculous situations as the cinema's cult of the anti-hero. It is now normal for films to conclude with the thief in some luxurious setting surrounded by money and women and no sign whatsoever of justice or retribution. It is acceptable for the individual to triumph over the perceived constraints of society, including its laws. And it is far more usual for the governments, police and similar bodies to be portrayed as corrupt, with 'hidden agendas' and secret conspiracies against you and me. And we have been brainwashed into cynically believing this to be normal.

A variant of the *Divine Command* notion of morality that does not require that you actually believe in God is to imagine what a perfectly good ruler, divine or otherwise, would do. Such an approach, used during the time of the Spanish Inquisition in the 15th century or the Puritan witch hunts in the 17th, might have prevented the horrific tortures and killings perpetrated in the name of God. It is, of course, still fallible as a justification for action since people may differ in their understanding of how a perfect being might act.

Yet another modern approach is to deem those actions to be good which are compatible with universal happiness. Kant's categorical imperative can then be modified to say that we should always act in such a way that it is commensurate with the possibility of universal happiness. With this simple premise, it is then obvious that such things as stealing and murder are wrong because they interfere with someone's right to seek their own happiness. But would the murder of someone like Hitler be justifiable in this sense?

Another modern approach is to attempt to quantify in some way all of the reasons for action or non-action. The idea is that asking what one should do is a request for information rather than an attempt to elicit actual advice from someone else or from God. We can then take account of all the relevant factors – what we will get out of it, how it will affect others, whether it is free and legal and so on. All of these can then be weighed up in a logical rather than emotive way and a reasoned conclusion reached.

An example of this has occurred to me recently. My mother-in-law was clearing out her attic and we took away several bags full of rubbish to dispose of. In sorting through this later, my wife discovered an old World War II print of a Robert Taylor painting of Lancaster Bombers, signed by Leonard Cheshire. (My father-in-law used to fly these airplanes.) A quick search on the Internet established that the signature alone was worth around £40, while Robert Taylor prints sold for anything from £50 upwards. On conducting a more detailed search the following day, I found the precise print listed at one specialist site, obviously no longer available other than by resale. It was valued at around £400.

What to do? My mother-in-law had thrown it out and, as far as she was concerned, it might now have been burned. Perhaps we should sell it and not tell her. This is the stance of the ethical egoist – do whatever is best for the agent (us). My wife thought that we should return it, or at least ask her mother's advice, and believed her mother should receive all proceeds. This is the position of the ethical altruist – do what is best for everyone except the agent. What I proposed is that we did not tell her until we had sold the print (so as not to raise her expectations) and then give her one third of the proceeds. My wife would have one third, for finding it, and I would have one third, for selling it. This is the 'Best Reasons' approach to moral decision making (and reflects my employment in the field of Software Metrics!).

As to what actually happened in this example: I sold it for only £50, having discovered that there were quite a few visible creases, which I had thought to be clouds! And my wife gave all of the money to her mother. This is according to the well-known principle whereby you research all of the relevant data to enable you to come to a reasoned conclusion and then your wife does what she had already decided to do in the first place. (Sorry, I lied – the money had already been used to pay bills before we even saw my mother-in-law!)

Free Will

Why do you act the way that you do? If it is because you feel you *ought* to do something, you probably recognize there is little free will involved. You are being 'coerced' by society or family, or influenced by concerns over what might happen if you don't act in that way. On the other hand, if you do something because you *want* to, then perhaps you believe you are exercising free will. But is this true even when you trace the source of your desire? For example, you see a cream cake in the window of a shop, and the thought arises, "I would like some cake." Did you freely choose to have that thought? Indeed, can you choose to have *any* thought? Do they not simply 'arise'?

Anyone who has thought deeply about spiritual matters knows that one of the fundamental problems is how to reconcile our day-to-day experience with claims about God or a non-dual reality. The first level seems concrete and demonstrable while the second is speculative, to say the least. Among the Indian philosophies, Advaita Vedanta is the only one that speaks of 'orders' of reality. There is the absolute non-dual reality; the empirical level – our day-to-day experience in the world; and the illusory level of dreams. Correctly differentiating among these levels is essential if we are to understand the subtleties involved in the question of free will.

The Western philosophical positions vary considerably. At the free-will end of the spectrum is the extreme **Libertarianism** of philosophers such as St. Augustine and Sartre. This says that as long as we are physically able to do something, have the opportunity to do it and are not constrained from doing it by some outside force, then we may freely choose to do it (or not) without anything, inside or out, 'making' us act one way or the other.

Universal determinism is the general belief that everything that happens does so necessarily as a result of the causes that precede it.

Theistic determinism (or *Predestination*) claims that these causes are the will of a God or gods. Some variants of this allow that we ourselves may have some free will within the overall constraints.

Fatalism is not quite the same thing. This maintains that some events (such as the time, place and nature of our death) are totally predetermined – nothing that we do can prevent these from happening – but for the rest of the time, the status quo is maintained.

Naturalistic determination is the belief that every event is the natural outcome of prior causes such as genetic and environmental factors (and that no god is involved). *Soft determinism* allows that some of these causes are our own desires, thoughts and feelings at the time of action (this is my own view). *Hard determinism* denies that our desires etc. play any part. This is the view of people like BF Skinner (he of the salivating dogs). Whether or not our own desire influences an action or not is how Aristotle differentiates actions. If the cause of an action is external and we do not contribute anything to it, then it is 'involuntary.' If the action is triggered by our personal desire or after appropriate deliberation about whether or not to act, then it is voluntary.

Compatibilism means that belief in both free will and determinism is not necessarily logically inconsistent (both libertarianism and hard determinism are therefore 'incompatibilist' beliefs). The crucial, practical aspect here is that compatibilism makes moral responsibility meaningful, whereas it is not meaningful for incompatibilism.

The manner in which we form habits shows how there may not be such a thing as free will. Edward de Bono's metaphor of pouring hot water onto jelly explains how this operates. The first time that we do this, the water will make faint channels in the surface of the jelly. The next time, there will be a tendency for the water to flow into those same channels. With repetition, over time the channels will become deep and it will be very difficult to get the water to flow anywhere else. This is how habitual modes of behavior come into being. We can employ willpower to overcome these habits and forge a new path, but it is not easy.

My own experience has convinced me that I do not have free will. As regards the trivial things in life, such as whether to have a cup of tea or coffee, if it is not habit that dictates the decision, it is availability, convenience, convention, and any number of other external factors. More significant aspects, affecting our future lives, are nevertheless similarly influenced by more important elements such as educational and social background, acquired skills, knowledge and qualifications etc. I truly believe that, if we analyze any decision that we make, whether irrelevant or life-changing, we will be able to trace many of the factors which led to the choice, and acknowledge the existence of innumerable others of which we are not immediately aware. By no stretch of the meaning of language can we really call this 'free' will.

Science tends to support claims that we don't have free will. The experiments of Benjamin Libet (reported in *Behavioral and Brain Sciences*, 1985) and Daniel Wegner (*American Psychologist*, 1999) demonstrate that what we feel to be a conscious decision to act actually takes place in the brain *after* the action has already been initiated as a result of mechanical cause-effect processes. It is as though, after the initial input X, there are two separate neurological paths. There is a subconscious process whereby X directly causes the action A. Quite separately, X gives rise to the conscious thought Y, which is followed by the decision to act D. Because D occurs before A, we imagine that D *causes* A, and thus have the illusion of free will.

Practically speaking, this does not change anything (few people are even aware of these experiments). But the implications are quite significant. We believe we are these bodies and minds, but we are not. They carry on quite happily without interference. They are simply waves, rising and falling on the ocean of consciousness. The problems arise when we *identify* with them. Although already free, perfect, complete, and unlimited, we then believe ourselves to be suffering individuals trapped in imperfect and mortal frames.

And this resolves the seeming paradox of free will. Whether or not we are deemed to have it depends upon the viewpoint we are adopting. It is actually the body-mind of matter that acts and suffers the consequences of those actions. The sense of free will is a part of that system. Accordingly, if we are identified with the body, we will seem to have free will and be subject to the law of cause and effect (what Eastern philosophies call 'karma'). From the standpoint of Consciousness, the ultimate sense of 'I', I can say that "I *have* a body but I am *not* the body." Neither am I the mind, and free will is only a concept in the mind. Karma relates to the body-mind and not to the real Self.

Another helpful way to think about it is in terms of the extent that we are in the present and directing our attention. If we are 'miles away', we inevitably do things in a habitual mechanical manner. On the other hand, if we are alert, there is an opportunity for the discriminating faculty of the mind to choose between various possible courses of action, depending on which action we perceive as most appropriate. Although this act of choosing may still be mechanical in the sense that it is determined by what we have learned in the past, the nature of the action is clearly quite different. In stillness, other factors, such as morality, can also influence the outcome. Discrimination, as opposed to habit, becomes the driving force. Therefore, the optimum way to 'act' is to be in the present, with a still mind, so that discrimination may operate and make the correct (if not actually 'free') choice.

As Spinoza said, *"Men believe themselves to be free, because they are conscious of their own actions and are ignorant of the causes by which they are determined."*

Belief

Belief can be a dangerous thing, as was mentioned earlier, regarding Galileo! And we also often tend to overestimate the value of a belief (as did the Inquisition in respect of Galileo!). It is so often treated by the believer as if it were true knowledge, instead of simply a strongly (and often wrongly!) held opinion. We really ought to know better, given the history of such mistaken, scientific views as the theories of phlogiston and ether. If the most brilliant scientists can be wrong, so can we!

Take, for example, the belief that people's behavior is influenced by a full moon. The problem is that people are selective in what they observe. They tend to notice things that support their present beliefs and, whenever they see something unusual, they tend to try to find an explanation. Thus, if someone is seen to be behaving in an abnormal manner and it is noticed that the moon happens to be full, the latter is likely to be used to explain the former, in the absence of any more rational explanation. Such rationalizations may become so glib that, in an appropriate situation, we may not even bother to check the phase of the moon at all. And, of course, we will recall those situations when something unusual occurred and it happened to be a full moon, but fail to remember the many more situations when either it was a full moon and everything was perfectly normal or it was not a full moon and people were doing the most stupid things!

Many of our beliefs stem from childhood. We are told something by our parents (who, of course, were told this by their parents!) and, not knowing any better, and trusting them implicitly, we accept it. If this happens to be something that does not fall within the purview of education, it is very likely that we will reach adulthood still believing what we were told. This is the field of folklore. Thus, for example, we might be told: *don't go out in the cold with wet hair or you will catch your death of cold!* And we believe it! Although there is no scientific evidence whatsoever for such a claim, that is irrelevant. The most pervasive belief of this kind is one's religious persuasion. If the Muslim child is brought up as a Christian, she will believe in Christianity – and vice versa. She may later be converted but then, one assumes, critical reason comes into play. Normally, the desirability of applying reason to one's beliefs rarely occurs to us. As Robert Bolton said: *"A belief is not merely an idea the mind possesses; it is an idea that possesses the mind."*

Ultimately, it could be said that *"we believe whatever we want to believe"*, as the Greek statesman Demosthenes said. The rebel mystic Osho has a good joke to illustrate this:

A man was driving home from work one night in the pouring rain when he passed a young woman struggling with some shopping. He stopped and offered her a lift. When they got to her house, she invited him in for a coffee. One thing led to another and, eventually, they ended up in bed making love. Much later, he got up to return home realizing that his wife was going to be demanding a good explanation. By the time he arrived home he had worked out what to do and he took a piece of chalk from the glove compartment and put it behind his ear. As soon as he entered the house, his wife loudly demanded to know where he had been all of this time.

"Well, darling," he began, "I stopped to give this girl a lift home. She invited me in for coffee and then we went to bed for a couple of hours."

"I've never heard so much rubbish," his wife replied. "I know perfectly well what you've been up to. You've been out with the boys playing pool again; I can see that chalk behind your ear!"

Consciousness

Modern philosophers have dubbed consciousness the 'hard

problem.' How is it possible for a material brain to have what we call 'subjective experience'? Our own lives and those of every philosopher and scientist who has gone before are simply incompatible with the idea that we are essentially matter in which, inexplicably, consciousness has somehow 'emerged.' And yet this is what most of them still claim.

The problem, as I see it, is simple: we need to differentiate between Consciousness and awareness. Consciousness enables the brain to perceive just as electricity enables the computer to process data. The computer does not generate electricity; the brain does not produce Consciousness.

Ever since the 'study' of consciousness began to be an academically acceptable area of research amongst scientists, both they and Western philosophers have been heading deeper and deeper into a conceptual cul-de-sac. At the root of the problem is the tacit assumption that science will (one day) be able to provide an explanation for everything. But, more specifically as regards this particular issue, the big 'C' of Consciousness must be differentiated from the little 'a' of awareness. The conflation of the two means that the true nature of Consciousness will forever elude them.

Below, I address some of the various misconceptions that are misleading many of the neuroscientists and philosophers in the field of Consciousness Studies. It is accepted that not all of these investigators will hold such 'extreme' positions (and a few are much more liberal in their approach).

The most fundamental but erroneous assumption is that Consciousness is somehow a 'product' of the brain, and that it 'resides' in its physical structure – it has 'neuronal correlates.' At some point in evolution, so the story goes, the brain acquired sufficient complexity and sophistication for this to occur. Being 'conscious' clearly confers an evolutionary advantage upon those animals which 'possess' it, so this makes perfect sense.

If it was simply a matter of seeing threats or potential mates, and reacting automatically like a computer program, then perhaps that would be good enough. But of course there is more to it than this. We are also aware of emotions which result from the sensory input. While the parts of the brain responsible for processing the input and output may be monitored and interfered with, what goes on with respect to our 'experience' of those things is rather less amenable to investigation.

But even this is confusing the issue. Emotions are certainly different in nature from perceptions but so, we might add, are thoughts. The entire problem can be simplified by saying that we are 'aware' of all of these things – objects in the world, physical feelings in the body, emotions and thoughts in the mind etc. And we could say (humor me for a while) that Consciousness is what enables us to do all of these things. 'Consciousness', operating through the brain, enables us to be 'aware.' Consciousness is not *generated* by the brain; rather it is the makeup of the brain which enables Consciousness to *manifest* in all those ways with which we are familiar. (Note that I am capitalizing 'Consciousness' to differentiate 'my' definition from that tacitly assumed by the scientist.)

Inanimate objects and simple life-forms do not 'exhibit' Consciousness – 'manifest' is a much more appropriate verb – but the manner in which they fail to manifest Consciousness is analogous to the way that faulty electrical equipment fails to manifest electricity. When a toaster or a radio is broken, electricity no longer has any effect on the mechanisms and the associated functions no longer operate. There is nothing mysterious here; we don't conclude that the electricity is no longer there or, worse still, that it is no longer being generated. When the brain is irreparably damaged or dead, Consciousness no longer has any effect on the mechanism and the 'person' is no longer present. It is not that Consciousness has 'gone'; the brain did not itself generate this.

Scientists only associate *complex* life-forms with consciousness and this leads them to such conclusions as that 'consciousness can be generated by either cortical hemisphere.' But does a severed head with an undamaged cortical hemisphere(s) manifest consciousness? Does a whole, but recently deceased, body (including head and cortex)? This obvious but telling observation seems to be studiously avoided by the worshippers of the neuron.

When we say that we are conscious, what we really mean is that we are aware of something. It is an indication that Consciousness is operating in the perceptual/conceptual regions of the brain. When we are driving a car 'on autopilot' and totally unaware of the surroundings, Consciousness is obviously still functioning, since the appropriate motor functions still operate to get us home.

This confusion of awareness and Consciousness leads to the most remarkable conclusions, such as that 'subconscious' activities such as this (performing actions 'automatically', while thinking or dreaming about something else entirely) are carried out *without* Consciousness! Computers might be thought to carry out 'unconscious processing', but brains certainly do not.

Various experiments have been carried out which show that our eyes see things that we claim not to be aware of. It is concluded that the 'saccade' system, whereby our eyes are constantly scanning the environment, is carried out without consciousness. Again, one has to observe that something is activating the system; dead people do not move their eyes to monitor their environment. It is acknowledged that certain parts of the brain appear to be responsible for controlling aspects of the body, and that this takes place below the level of awareness; but this further highlights the confusion of terminology. There are so many aspects, from pumping the blood to tying our shoelaces, that it simply would not be possible to involve our so-called conscious mind in all of them! Some we learn and then relegate to autopilot; some we haven't even the slightest idea how to perform, such as regulating our body temperature. We are aware of very little but Consciousness is involved in everything.

The sensations that the brain is capable of experiencing do indeed depend upon the makeup of the brain and sense organs. We do not have the physical equipment to detect X-rays or radio waves without the assistance of technology but this is a limitation of our bodily equipment and has nothing to do with Consciousness. Examining the brain is always only going to be examining the equipment. Even if you could tell exactly what a person was feeling, perceiving and thinking, by analyzing their MRI scans for example, you would still know nothing about Consciousness.

It is not that man can experience more than dogs or plants because man has more Consciousness (as a result of having more neurons, a greater scope for connectivity etc.). It is that our brains can do more with the **same** Consciousness, just as a computer can 'do more' than a light bulb with the same electricity. Because human brains are so much more complex than those of the lower animals, scientists erroneously conclude that Consciousness has evolved, or is 'emergent' as the system evolves. The bigger the network, the greater is the number of states – true. But this is only analogous to, say, a more sophisticated amplifier having tuners and frequency analyzers, while the basic ones just have a volume control. It is the same electricity passing through both.

So many assumptions have been made in the history of consciousness studies, yet these have usually not been made 'consciously'! They are rarely even recognized as assumptions, being taken as self-evidently true. Thus, Consciousness is not a property of complex states, it happens to manifest in them. It is not a property of living matter. Vast amounts of effort have been expended over the past few decades trying to find its origin, assuming it to have a biological basis. No one would want to admit that this might not be so – a supreme example of cognitive dissonance if ever there was one!

So convinced are scientists that consciousness is somehow 'produced by' the brain that they can categorically state that there is no mysterious force separating organic and inorganic matter and that life is nothing more than physics and chemistry.

Yet they are forced to acknowledge that experience is not a material thing and cannot be explained by physical properties of the brain. This is the 'hard problem' of what they call 'qualia', the 'units' of experience – what it 'feels like' to perceive objects in the world. Maybe we can indeed say that qualia are 'features of matter' or 'properties of the world' but this does not mean that Consciousness is as well. Consciousness is what enables matter (i.e. brains) to have experiences.

Finding out what it is that determines whether X is able to have qualia is not going to tell us anything about Consciousness. The extent to which insects are self-aware, or whether it is possible or even meaningful for computers to be aware, are interesting questions, but futile ones as far as understanding Consciousness is concerned.

The bottom line is always going to be that Consciousness is not amenable to investigation at all. It is 'I' who has experiences, and 'I' am always the subject. (I only have your word for the fact that you have experiences, too. Your word and even your very existence are simply further elements of my experience.) We are conscious of our body and our minds in the same way that we are conscious of gross objects in the outside world. Our own brain is just as much an object as the apple or the house; I just can't see it quite so easily. 'I' can never investigate this 'I' using the objective methods of science because 'I', the subject, would always be the one looking. 'I' am not measurable; I am the one doing the measuring.

Without Consciousness, nothing can be known. But Consciousness itself cannot be an object of knowledge, just as in a totally dark room, a torch may illuminate everything but itself. Knowing requires both knower and known. For Consciousness to be known, it would have to be a knowable object, but it is the knowing subject. We 'know' Consciousness because we are Consciousness. Consciousness is our true nature. The ultimate observer (which is who you essentially are) is simply not amenable to any type of objective investigation: who could there be beyond the ultimate observer to do the investigating?

Numerous attempts have been made to define Consciousness. Most seem to revolve around the assumption that a person's behavior indicates its presence or absence. It is argued that consciousness is present during the waking and dream states but not in deep sleep or under anesthesia, for example. But this is again to confuse Consciousness and awareness. When we awake from a deep sleep, we are able to state with confidence that we were 'aware of nothing.' This is a positive statement – there were no gross objects, emotions or thoughts present for us to perceive.

It is analogous to the astronaut in deep space facing away from the sun. There is nothing to reflect the sunlight so only blackness is seen. But the sun is still present, just as Consciousness is still present in sleep. If this were not so, what would cause it to reappear on awakening? And why could dead people not also regain consciousness? We must also differentiate Consciousness from 'being conscious'!

It is not possible to have a behavioral definition. If someone responds to a question or command (even if this response can only be determined by MRI scan), it shows that their body-mind is 'animated' by Consciousness, but it cannot say anything about what Consciousness is. All that we can say is that the person is conscious (to some degree). An analogy would be to try to claim that, because we can observe an automobile moving, we therefore understand the nature of petrol. Examining the brain in the ways described by neurobiology is like tinkering with the carburetor or spark plug timing – it will certainly influence how the petrol functions but you cannot thereby determine its chemical formula.

Supposedly, one of the more illuminating avenues for investigating consciousness is the observation of the behavior and analysis of the brain functions of those people with brain damage of one sort or another. A metaphor for this might be the way in which light is reflected by a dirty or cracked mirror. Looking into such a mirror, the quality of the reflection would clearly depend upon the nature of the dirt or damage. But, just as this could tell us nothing about light, so the brain-damaged can tell us nothing about Consciousness.

Accidents, infections, scalpels may all affect the brain and cause changes in perception, cognition etc. Clearly the brain is responsible for all of the differentiating aspects of consciousness. But what is happening is that Consciousness remains the same but is unable to function in those areas which have been damaged. It is like a complex model railway. The locomotive is itself independent of, and unaffected by, the railway track but it can no longer reach those stations to which parts of the track have been damaged or removed.

Of course, metaphors often help us to reach an intuitive understanding of something which is inherently complex, but they can also mislead. I have used the analogies of electricity and light above but both of these are essentially material in nature – we can point to electrons and photons, respectively. What must be avoided is disposing of the neuroscientist as a candidate for understanding Consciousness and instead sending the particle physicist off down a blind alley in search of the C particle! Despite what scientists insist must be the case, Consciousness is subjective; this means not objective, and this equates to immaterial – not matter.

In summary, then, the brain is only a medium through which Consciousness manifests. The more complex the brain, the more sophisticated the perception and behavior can be. But, just as examining a mirror will not provide an understanding of the nature of the sun, so all of the efforts made by the neuroscientist will tell us nothing about the nature of Consciousness.

In order to understand (as far as is possible) what exactly Consciousness is, we have to look in an entirely different direction, one which is intrinsically closed to science. One might call this 'philosophy' but philosophers, too, are not immune to the pitfall of objectivity. Rather it is an understanding that arises as a result of a guided investigation into the Self (the ultimate observer, the subject rather than any object). One such proven system is the teaching of Advaita, a branch of Indian philosophy that was systematized over 1,200 years ago. Unfortunately (and this is not a cop-out!), it is not possible to convince you of this in a few sentences. Read my books!

Conclusions

So, did any of these philosophies provide me with the answers for which I had been looking? Clearly not, since all of the books that I have written have been on or around the non-dualistic Hindu philosophy of Advaita Vedanta. But naturally truth seekers often tend to reach similar conclusions so it is not surprising that there are aspects that coincide. Also, since Vedantic philosophy is much older than Western, it is inevitable that some Westerners were influenced by contact with the East, whether direct or indirect.

This has also been a very cursory overview and obviously much has been omitted, particularly the ideas of more recent philosophers. But I must remind the reader that I have not studied any of these philosophers in any depth and my findings are the result of reading histories, dictionaries and overviews and of research on the Internet, rather than original material. I have extracted only those ideas that seemed relevant to my 'search for meaning.'

Philosophers typically take an interest in many areas, even if they concentrate principally on just one or two and they often devote much effort to supporting, or more frequently refuting, the ideas of their predecessors. If you should attempt to go into any significant detail on aspects outlined above, you will soon find yourself reading many books and studying often complex arguments on all sides of the issue. All that I attempted to do was to find some relevant ideas and I have to say that none of the ones that I discovered seem entirely appropriate for today's society.

Certainly it was clear that the School of Economic Science had not taken its influence from any of these sources. Some of the ideas did resonate. For example, the idea that the empirical world is constantly changing (Heraclitus) but that there must be some underlying 'reality' that is unitary and never changes (Parmenides). People's lives seem to be ruled by ignorance and yet there also seems to be some innate understanding of the finer principles of life, such as truth and justice (Socrates and Plato). 'Know thyself' must be the most fundamental guidance for giving a life meaning and purpose.

In our philosophical investigations, we have to be guided by the findings and thoughts of those who have gone before, but we must use reason at each step of the way to question and reflect upon what others say, even though we trust them not to deceive us deliberately (Aristotle). Possessions do not bring lasting happiness – a pauper may be happier than a king. We have somehow to seek happiness 'within' (Cynics).

Some of the movements in Greek philosophy effectively just accepted that this life was all there is. It may not be ideal by a long way but there are things we can do to make it more bearable. We can even simply pursue pleasure as an end in itself, accepting that there will be times when pain has to be substituted (Cynics, Skeptics, Epicureans, Stoics). For someone who has already rejected life as an 'end in itself', however, who is unable to derive satisfaction at the social pleasure-in-the-moment level, this attitude is not possible. It would also be a totally defeatist stance, knowing that many have looked and found meaning beyond such transitory experiences.

None of the mediaeval philosophers struck a chord, concerned as most of them were with problems of Christianity. I had never felt able to believe in a separate god or a heaven. These ideas were so 'anti-scientific', and my education was very much based in science. When I was forced, as a small child, to attend Sunday School at a Methodist church, I remember arguing with my parents at one stage, saying that, if there was a god, he had to be everywhere. If he was far away in some other place then he could not be the all-powerful, ever-present entity that was claimed. Even then, I was putting reason ahead of faith when it came to assessing claims outside of my experience!

Having been educated as a scientist, I was naturally impressed with how much was explained by science – obviously with far more still to come. But… matter may have been broken down, first into atoms, then into protons, neutrons and electrons, then mesons, then quarks, then…? There was still no explanation of the fundamental nature of reality.

Descartes' mind-body duality left too many unanswered questions and bringing god into the problem of causality did not solve anything for me! More appealing was the notion that there are not really any 'separate individuals' at all but that, somehow, we are all one and the same. To be a 'part' of god would not solve this, since we would still be effectively separate. Indeed, having god *and* us did not work either, since there would still be the inevitability of acting in accord with, or against, god's will. None of the various views seemed to resolve all these objections.

Of all the Western philosophy I have researched, Spinoza comes closest to addressing what I believe 'really matters.' His aim was to attain to *"knowledge of the union existing between the mind and the whole of Nature"* and he deemed anything to be 'good' that helped him along this path to perfect his character. His conclusions that it was pointless to look for happiness and that we did not have free will both accorded with my own views.

The conclusions of Locke (and later, Kant) that we are only ever aware of the qualities, or attributes, of objects and never of the primary substance of which they are formed was a fundamental one for me. I may see a red object in front of me and you may see a green one, but we might both call it 'blue' because our upbringing and education have taught us that 'blue' is the name conventionally given to the wavelength of the color that we are perceiving. In fact, this process goes much deeper and it was not until I understood the teaching of Advaita much later that I appreciated how fundamental this is. It is even convention that dictates how we configure the forms that we perceive. We are taught to give specific names to particular forms and the language then shapes our perception. The only thing we can be sure of, said Locke and Descartes, and I had to agree, is our own existence.

Berkeley's Idealism comes closest of the Western philosophies to expressing the nature of reality but suffers from the counterintuitive way in which it is presented. It is difficult to argue against the position that 'objects' as we perceive them are effectively in the mind. Kant subsequently demonstrated how we can never see the 'things in themselves' only their attributes, which are merely impressions received through the senses. But to speak of objects having a 'real' existence in the 'mind of god' was, to my mind, a step too far (obviously so for a nonbeliever!).

As I already noted above, Kant promoted several ideas which I considered particularly noteworthy, not least his differentiation of the empirical world in which we live from the forever-hidden reality which is its substrate. His 'Categorical Imperative' and suggestion that we act because it is the 'right thing to do' rather than for desired outcome also sounded eminently reasonable.

Hegel's idea of a unitary 'Absolute', beginningless and endless, was appealing but his notion that it was constantly evolving seemed contradictory. Surely if it was 'absolute', it must also be infinite and already 'perfect' and complete. How could it 'change' into something better? His 'dialectic' process might be fine for the (apparent) practical world but seemed meaningless in terms of the reality. In fact, the development and subsequent decline of Communism indicates that the theory did not really work in the empirical realm either. Both he and Marx do not seem to go far enough in their differentiation of 'reality' and 'world.' If the statement I made above, that Marx thought we could *"monitor the dialectic process (of reality) by studying history"* is true, then this is a clear confusion of real and apparent. History relates to the apparent world, not to reality, so anything in the world can tell us nothing about the real.

As I have already mentioned, Schopenhauer's thinking has much in common with Eastern (Vedic) philosophy, so it is no surprise in retrospect that some of his ideas had particular resonance for me. Indeed, I have to confess that my brief 'summary' earlier was couched in terms that I *now* understand to be the case rather than in words that he might have used.

The 'language' philosophers may have been essentially diverted from the true purpose of philosophy but they had hit upon a valuable observation. In a real sense, the way in which we used language molded the way in which we viewed the world. Of course, the Chandogya Upanishad from around 600–800BC had made this point even more strongly. We shape gold into a form that can be worn on the finger; we call this a 'ring' and treat it as though it were a new object entirely. But it always has been and always will be only 'gold.' Merleau-Ponty acknowledged that we are unable to see the world as it is because of the inescapable subjective nature of our perception. But he still believed that we are our bodies…

Somehow, Western philosophies leave a feeling of incompleteness or even emptiness. Maybe they provide excellent guidelines for discriminating between potential courses of action in a specific situation but there is no overall sense of purpose and meaning. If I want to know whether I ought to go out to the cinema or visit my ageing grandmother, there is much material to provide guidance – in fact, I could decide to stay in and read all about it for the next few weeks instead of going anywhere. But when it comes to giving me a raison d'être for my life, it seems that, unless I adopt a religious outlook and acquire faith in a heaven and hell, I am left with little of substance.

According to the twentieth century philosopher Karl Popper, we can never be sure of anything in the sense of a proven scientific fact – certainty does not exist. Newton's laws were regarded as certain in this way and the scientific world was shaken when Einstein showed that they did not apply to the very small or very fast. And this is how it has to be. Though we cannot prove theories, we can show them to be wrong. The classic example relates to the one-time belief that all swans are white. No amount of observing swans and seeing them to be white could prove this to be true but as soon as a black swan was found the theory was immediately shown to be false.

Happiness

For me, Schopenhauer summed it up very simply: *"It is difficult to find happiness in oneself, but it is impossible to find it anywhere else."*

Since you 'chose' to read this book, I suggest that there is a high probability that you are not happy! It is an undeniable fact that the majority of people today are dissatisfied with what they perceive as being a mediocre existence. They may feel that they are limited by an unattractive and illness-prone body or by a mind that is imperfectly educated and unable to make intellectual leaps of understanding. There are very many things that we want – objects, partners, lifestyle, jobs etc. – but few that we seem to be able to obtain. (And, even when we do obtain them, their rewards are invariably ephemeral.) Western society relies upon the media advertising all of these things, and thereby continually reinforcing the desires. Being repeatedly frustrated by this materialistic lifestyle, it should be hardly surprising that many turn towards the spiritual in the hope that this might bring about peace and a durable happiness.

The problem is that all 'paths' and 'systems' can only promise us a *future* happiness, so that we need to have some sort of reassurance that the commitment of our time and effort will prove worthwhile. Unfortunately, the majority of the 'new age' techniques bring with them no reassurance at all. Frequently, these systems are quite contrary to reason and often rely upon putting one's belief into something that is totally unbelievable. Cynically, one might think that the only reason that there are *several* books upon a particular topic is that the later authors realized after the first book that there was money to be made out of a gullible public.

A 'spiritual seeker' might be defined as the person who has realized that the attaining of 'things' does not, in fact, bring about lasting happiness. All it does is trigger the beginning of the next desire. This is what leads people to seek the magical, the fantastical that will shatter our mundane existence once and for all. Whether this be foretelling our future through tea leaves or crystals, or communicating with aliens or angels hardly matters; our minds make the leap from the worldly to the unknowable, other world where we are promised something that will truly satisfy.

But of course it doesn't, because such worlds are not only unknowable but also imaginary. The fact that this cannot be proven to be so allows such ideas to exist but makes no difference to the outcome. Desiring the illusory is ultimately no more satisfying than obtaining the desirable.

We need to think about what it is that we really want and then refine our desires; evolving from wanting mere gross objects to the desire to discover our own nature and that of reality itself. It is discovered that our desires develop from the gross to the more refined. There is a natural and a necessary progression involved here. We begin with wanting simply *things* in the outside world (of course these may be people or situations etc.). Then we realize that it is not the things themselves that we want but the happiness that we believe they will bring. The objects are many but the happiness is actually only one. Moreover, there usually comes a time when the object ceases to give happiness and you want to get rid of it!

The next step follows logically from the previous. The fact that things do not always give happiness means that the happiness is not actually in the object but in our self. It is never anywhere else! And it is this fact that deserves serious investigation. The suggestion is that happiness is our natural state and that this is revealed whenever a desire is removed (e.g. when we obtain something that we want and the desire for it goes away). Clearly, since we do not experience happiness all the time, this natural state must somehow be covered over. So the next startling realization is that nothing I can *do* could ever obtain happiness for me (since I cannot choose whether or not to have desires). Indeed, it seems that most of the things that I do bring unhappiness! Instead, what has to happen is that I must come to know this natural state, i.e. my true self. This true self is not something to be obtained but something I have to know. Accordingly, the penultimate refinement of my desires is from wanting to find my Self to wanting Self-knowledge.

And thus we come to Advaita. Advaita is a proven teaching methodology to give me knowledge of my Self. The knowledge is contained in the scriptures called the Upanishads, which were written down thousands of years ago, having previously been passed down by word of mouth from the ancient sages. Since they were necessarily in fairly dense form, and written in Sanskrit, they need to be interpreted and explained by someone who both knows the Self and is familiar with the techniques, stories and metaphors used to unfold these scriptures. These techniques have themselves been passed down from guru to disciple in a structured manner. Accordingly, the last refinement is from wanting knowledge, to wanting to hear these scriptures explained by a qualified teacher.

So, what does Advaita actually say? Very briefly, we presently experience ourselves as separate persons in a universe of objects. Despite this seeming duality, according to Advaita, reality is actually non-dual. This non-dual reality is called Brahman. As a matter of fact we do feel ourselves to be other than our body or mind. Advaita calls our essential self, which is beyond body and mind, the Atman. And the fundamental message of the Upanishads is that this Atman is Brahman.

There is an oft-quoted sentence which is said to summarize Advaita. This is:

brahma satyam, jaganmithya, jivo brahmaiva naparah

(this is the Romanized equivalent of that Sanskrit sentence). Translated, it means: "Brahman is the reality; the world is not in itself real; the individual self is not different from Brahman." And the purpose of the teaching is simply to bring about this realization.

Unlike religions and most other spiritual systems, you are not asked to set aside reason and accept the unprovable as truth. On the contrary, you are encouraged to question everything until all doubts are satisfied. The only 'practices' you are expected to follow are those which promote self-control of mind and senses so that discrimination may operate in a still mind. Thereafter, it is simply a matter of listening or reading, clarifying confusion and reflecting until there is 'enlightenment.'

Following the period of maybe 2–3 years, in which I browsed the Western philosophies, I spent maybe 15–20 years studying Advaita in depth. I applied doubt and reason to a greater extent because of an innate suspicion regarding anything that assigns so much significance to ancient writings. I can claim with certainty that Advaita provides the answers that Western philosophy has not.

Further reading about Advaita

- Short book for complete beginners – *Advaita Made Easy* (2012).
- For those who already know a little – *The Book of One: The Ancient Wisdom of Advaita* (2003), extensively revised in 2010.
- The encyclopedic book using quotations from many teachers – *Back to the Truth: 5000 years of Advaita* (2007).
- Why traditional teaching is best – *Enlightenment: The Path Through The Jungle* (2008).
- A readable commentary on possibly the most profound Advaita text – *A-U-M: Awakening to Reality* (2015).
- And for an extended, autobiographical discussion on my search for meaning and purpose, via sociology, Western philosophy, science, and eventually Advaita: *How to Meet Yourself... and find true happiness* (2007).

Endnote

† The words 'ethics' and 'morality' are often used interchangeably. The former is perhaps better used to refer to a specific theory or set of principles defining things such as good and evil and ideal patterns of human behavior. 'Morals' more appropriately refer to nominally accepted, practical rules defining whether we ought to do A or B in a particular life situation.

BOOKS

Iff Books

ACADEMIC AND SPECIALIST

Iff Books publishes non-fiction. It aims to work with authors
and titles that augment our understanding of the human
condition, society and civilisation, and the world or universe in
which we live.
If you have enjoyed this book, why not tell other readers by
posting a review on your preferred book site.

Recent bestsellers from Iff Books are:

Why Materialism Is Baloney
How True Skeptics Know There is no Death and Fathom
Answers to Life, the Universe, and Everything
Bernardo Kastrup
A hard-nosed, logical, and skeptic non-materialist metaphysics,
according to which the body is in mind, not mind in the body.
Paperback: 978-1-78279-362-5 ebook: 978-1-78279-361-8

The Fall
Steve Taylor
The Fall discusses human achievement versus the issues of war,
patriarchy and social inequality.
Paperback: 978-1-90504-720-8 ebook: 978-184694-633-2

Brief Peeks Beyond
Critical Essays on Metaphysics, Neuroscience, Free Will,
Skepticism and Culture
Bernardo Kastrup
An incisive, original, compelling alternative to current
mainstream cultural views and assumptions.
Paperback: 978-1-78535-018-4 ebook: 978-1-78535-019-1

Framespotting
Changing How You Look at Things Changes How
You See Them
Laurence & Alison Matthews
A punchy, upbeat guide to framespotting. Spot deceptions and
hidden assumptions; swap growth for growing up. See and be
free.
Paperback: 978-1-78279-689-3 ebook: 978-1-78279-822-4

Is There an Afterlife?

David Fontana

Is there an Afterlife? If so what is it like? How do Western ideas of the afterlife compare with Eastern? David Fontana presents the historical and contemporary evidence for survival of physical death.

Paperback: 978-1-90381-690-5

Nothing Matters

A Book About Nothing

Ronald Green

Thinking about Nothing opens the world to everything by illuminating new angles to old problems and stimulating new ways of thinking.

Paperback: 978-1-84694-707-0 ebook: 978-1-78099-016-3

Panpsychism

The Philosophy of the Sensuous Cosmos

Peter Ells

Are free will and mind chimeras? This book, anti-materialistic but respecting science, answers: No! Mind is foundational to all existence.

Paperback: 978-1-84694-505-2 ebook: 978-1-78099-018-7

Punk Science

Inside the Mind of God

Manjir Samanta-Laughton

Many have experienced unexplainable phenomena; God, psychic abilities, extraordinary healing and angelic encounters. Can cutting-edge science actually explain phenomena previously thought of as 'paranormal'?

Paperback: 978-1-90504-793-2

The Vagabond Spirit of Poetry
Edward Clarke
Spend time with the wisest poets of the modern age and of the past, and let Edward Clarke remind you of the importance of poetry in our industrialized world.
Paperback: 978-1-78279-370-0 ebook: 978-1-78279-369-4

Readers of ebooks can buy or view any of these bestsellers by clicking on the live link in the title. Most titles are published in paperback and as an ebook. Paperbacks are available in traditional bookshops. Both print and ebook formats are available online.

Find more titles and sign up to our readers' newsletter at http://www.johnhuntpublishing.com/non-fiction

Follow us on Facebook at https://www.facebook.com/JHPNonFiction
and Twitter at https://twitter.com/JHPNonFiction